Plough Quarterly

BREAKING GROUND FOR A RENEWED WORLD

Summer 2019, Number 21

Artists: Wassily Kandinsky, N. C. Wyeth, Deborah Batt, Kari Nielsen, Chris Arnade, William Morris, Hilzías Salazar, Amedeo Modigliani, Benjamin Meader, Bianca Berends, Elise Palmigiani, Danny Burrows

WWW.PLOUGH.COM

Plough Quarterly

WWW.PLOUGH.COM

Meet the community behind *Plough*

Plough Quarterly is published by the Bruderhof, an international community of families and singles seeking to follow Jesus together. Members of the Bruderhof are committed to a way of radical discipleship in the spirit of the Sermon on the Mount. Inspired by the first church in Jerusalem (Acts 2 and 4), they renounce private property and share everything in common in a life of nonviolence, justice, and service to neighbors near and far. The community includes people from a wide range of backgrounds. There are twenty-three Bruderhof settlements in both rural and urban locations in the United States, England, Germany, Australia, and Paraguay, with around 3,000 people in all.

To learn more or arrange a visit, see the community's website at *bruderhof.com.*

Plough Quarterly features original stories, ideas, and culture to inspire everyday faith and action. Starting from the conviction that the teachings and example of Jesus can transform and renew our world, we aim to apply them to all aspects of life, seeking common ground with all people of goodwill regardless of creed. The goal of *Plough Quarterly* is to build a living network of readers, contributors, and practitioners so that, in the words of Hebrews, we may "spur one another on toward love and good deeds."

Plough Quarterly includes contributions that we believe are worthy of our readers' consideration, whether or not we fully agree with them. Views expressed by contributors are their own and do not necessarily reflect the editorial position of *Plough* or of the Bruderhof communities.

Editors: Peter Mommsen, Veery Huleatt, Sam Hine. Creative director: Clare Stober. Designers: Rosalind Stevenson, Miriam Burleson. Managing editor: Shana Goodwin. Associate editors: Maureen Swinger, Susannah Black.
Founding editor: Eberhard Arnold (1883–1935).
Plough Quarterly No. 21: Beyond Capitalism
Published by Plough Publishing House, ISBN 978-0-87486-306-2
Copyright © 2019 by Plough Publishing House. All rights reserved.

Scripture quotations (unless otherwise noted) are from the New Revised Standard Version Bible, copyright © 1989 the Division of Christian Education of the National Council of the Churches of Christ in the United States of America. Used by permission. All rights reserved.

Front cover: *ATM* by Paweł Kuczyński; image used with permission. Back cover: Photograph by @mckellajo from Hive & Hum. Inside front cover: Image from WikiArt (public domain).

Editorial Office
151 Bowne Drive
Walden, NY 12586
T: 845.572.3455
info@plough.com

Subscriber Services
PO Box 345
Congers, NY 10920-0345
T: 800.521.8011
subscriptions@plough.com

United Kingdom
Brightling Road
Robertsbridge
TN32 5DR
T: +44(0)1580.883.344

Australia
4188 Gwydir Highway
Elsmore, NSW
2360 Australia
T: +61(0)2.6723.2213

Plough Quarterly (ISSN 2372-2584) is published quarterly by Plough Publishing House, PO Box 398, Walden, NY 12586.
Individual subscription $32 / £24 / €28 per year. Subscribers outside the United Kingdom and European Union pay in US dollars.
Periodicals postage paid at Walden, NY 12586 and at additional mailing offices.
POSTMASTER: Send address changes to *Plough Quarterly,* PO Box 345, Congers, NY 10920-0345.

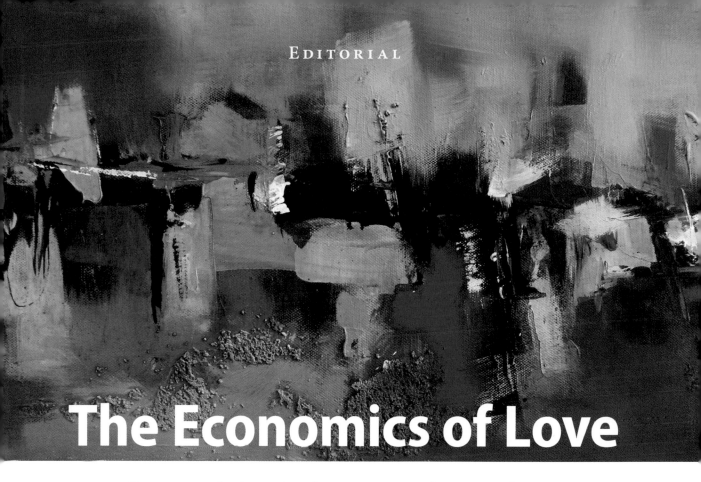

The Economics of Love

Beyond Capitalism – and Socialism

PETER MOMMSEN

Liberty, equality, fraternity: the promise of the French Revolution intoxicated twenty-one-year-old William Wordsworth. Looking back on that time, he penned a poem that famously evokes his generation's fervor. "Bliss was it in that dawn to be alive, / But to be young was very heaven!" He and his fellow radicals – "we who were strong in love" – felt sure they could make real change in the here and now: "not in Utopia . . . but in the very world, which is the world / Of all of us."

The young poet's ardor leaps out across the intervening centuries. In *The Prelude*, the 1805 poem in which these lines appear, the details of the French revolutionary program get scant attention. What matters is the sense of endless possibilities, the excitement of a "we" joining together to shape a new world.

That excitement is in the air again. A leading US presidential candidate espouses socialism, as does Britain's Leader of the Opposition. Europe's social democratic parties are hastening to reclaim their class-war roots so as to fend off far-left challengers. Membership in the Democratic Socialists of America has grown from six thousand in 2016 to around sixty thousand in 2019. According to a much-cited 2018 Gallup poll, 51 percent of Americans age eighteen to twenty-nine have a positive view of socialism (just 45 percent say the same of capitalism).

Today's radicals don't talk so much of bliss, at least to judge from the earnest pages of left

Artwork
by Elise
Palmigiani

All Things in Common

Peter Walpot (1521-1578), a Hutterite bishop, wrote a classic Anabaptist confession of faith, the Great Article Book, *from which this reading is taken.*

Property has no part in the Christian church; rather, it belongs to the world, it belongs to paganism, to those that do not have the love of God; it is proper to those that live according to their own will. If there were no self-will, there would be no property. True community of goods, on the other hand, is proper to believers, for by divine right, says Augustine, all things ought to be common, and no one should take to himself what is God's, any more than he would the air, rain, snow, or water, as well as the sun, the moon, and the elements. . . .

Whoever encloses and appropriates that which is, and should be, free, does so against Him who made and created it free, and it is sin. . . . But through men's acquired wickedness, through envy and greed everybody puts everything in his own pocket. The one says, "This is mine," and the other, "That is mine," and so a division has arisen among human beings, and great inequality has come into this life. Unfortunately, it has gone so far that, if they could grab hold of the sun and the moon and the elements, they would appropriate them and sell them for money.

Source: "True Surrender and Christian Community of Goods," Section 143, ed. Robert Friedmann, *Mennonite Quarterly Review*, January 1957.

journals like *Jacobin* and *In These Times*. Even so, there's a sense of newly opened possibilities: that now is the moment for the tyranny of concentrated power and wealth to be overcome by a mass movement of solidarity.

Socialism seems to mean different things to different individuals; as in Wordsworth's day, the details of a particular program don't appear to be what's driving the radical wave. Instead, what grips people is the liberating sense of finally having a cause to fight for.

But what exactly is this cause? Socialism's champions know how to take effective whacks at capitalism, and they get at least one thing right: the fact that we live in a society of immense affluence and desperate poverty is a public sin with which no person of good will can be at peace. Anyone who affirms the Golden Rule – "Do to others as you would have done to you" – is morally bound to strive for the same essentials of life for others that one desires for one's own family: health care, decent housing, education, a living wage, and security in old age. That millions lack these essentials in the richest civilization the world has ever known should shock the conscience.

But diagnosis is not yet the cure. Socialists grow coy when it comes to the realities of a state takeover of the entire economy. Bhaskar Sunkara's much-discussed book *The Socialist Manifesto*, for example, opens with a fun chapter, "A Day in the Life of a Socialist Citizen," that imagines an America in 2036 where wage labor has been abolished and the means of production are now owned by the government. This light-hearted depiction of a New Jersey pasta-sauce company called Bongiovi and a workers' revolution led by Bruce Springsteen is a far cry from real-world examples of socialist governance, such as the ongoing crisis in Venezuela. Thus this peek into an alternative future conveys the opposite of what it intends. We're invited to take it on faith that this time around, a happy conjunction of democracy and good intentions will somehow overcome socialism's long track record of sliding into dictatorship and repression.

Meanwhile, capitalism's malcontents on the right are equally hazy about ends and means. Many younger conservatives rightly deplore the ways capitalism is wrecking traditional bonds of solidarity, community, and family. They see capitalism's liberal elites aggressively sabotaging the values that give the lives of the working poor meaning and dignity: the institution of marriage, the bonds of faith, ideals of womanhood and manhood, loyalty to place, a sense of belonging. *First Things* magazine recently published a punchy manifesto that declares: "We oppose the soulless society of individual affluence. . . . We resist a tyrannical liberalism. . . . We want a country that works for workers."

This statement's signatories do have specific suggestions for how to edge toward these goals. Yet the contours of the eventual society that would truly fulfill their aspirations remain frustratingly vague. Proposals that circulate online – three-acres-and-a-cow distributism, Habsburg restoration – sound just as improbable as Marx's communist utopia.

In their indictments of capitalism, conservatives and socialists share some remarkable common ground, though of course their preferred remedies sharply diverge. Both stand against apologists for the present system such as the author Steven Pinker, who trumpet statistics showing rising per capita income, life expectancy, and personal freedom in order to accuse capitalism's critics of ingratitude. In response, the critics can point to other, grimmer statistics: in the world's wealthiest countries, rates of mental illness have jumped, while so-called deaths of despair from suicide and drug overdoses are reaching epidemic levels. Falling birth rates in countries with high standards of living seem to reflect pessimism about humanity's future. There's the looming risk of catastrophic climate change caused, in no small part, by capitalism. Is this, they ask, really what a human-friendly economy looks like?

Those eager for a life beyond capitalism must make a crucial decision: whether or not their main hope lies in grasping for the levers of government power. This is not the place for exploring the uses and limits of politics. But Christians especially should keep in mind the downsides inherent in any attempt to secure the common good through state coercion.

Any serious vision of the common good is anchored in moral convictions. Yet state imposition of moral convictions amounts to a state religion. (Martin Hägglund's call to socialism in his book *This Life* even calls it a "secular faith.") Whatever the creed – Robespierre's Cult of Reason, or Catholic integralism, or a progressive college's code of student conduct, or sharia law – the moment that it is backed by the sword of the state it will take on the role of Dostoyevsky's blasphemous Grand Inquisitor, offering cheap happiness in exchange for spiritual freedom.

Christians should fear assuming this role as a threat to their own integrity. Power corrupts religion from within by substituting coercion for free assent; the heavier the coercion exercised, the deeper the self-corruption. As the early church father Tertullian protested, "It is assuredly no part of religion to compel religion." To illustrate the two contrasting paths Christians can take, let's time-travel back to the spiritual roots of my own community, the

Bruderhof, in the Radical Reformation of the sixteenth century. At that time, the so-called Magisterial Reformers such as Martin Luther and John Calvin sought to purge the abuses of the medieval church by allying themselves with secular princes, using the power of the state to impose what they believed to be a purified gospel.

By contrast, the Radical Reformers emerged from a grassroots movement for justice among the common people. The peasants formulated their demands in Twelve Articles that are considered modern Europe's first human rights document. It included pleas to end cruel levels of taxation, tithing, and forced labor, as well as calls for commoners to be allowed to enjoy the bounty of creation, which originally had been given to all humankind: "It is unbrotherly and not in accordance with the word of God that the simple man does not have the right to catch game, fowl, and fish."

When peasant protests turned violent in 1525, both Luther and Catholic prelates pronounced God's blessing on the princes' bloody campaign of repression; an estimated one hundred thousand were killed. In the aftermath of this church-sanctioned mass murder, the Radical Reformation movement was born. Having learned hard lessons about taking up arms, its leaders (mostly) preached nonviolence. Yet their movement embodied the Twelve Articles' demand for brotherly community, now transformed by a Christian imagination. Because they insisted on voluntary baptism of adults rather than mandatory infant baptism, they were nicknamed Anabaptists ("re-baptizers"). Anabaptism was soon a capital crime throughout the Holy Roman Empire, and some three thousand Anabaptists were executed in the following decades.

Nevertheless, the movement spread. Around 1527, Anabaptists in present-day Czechia started forming communal settlements in which, following the example of the first Christians, members held all things in common. By century's end, there were about one hundred such settlements, with twenty to thirty thousand inhabitants living in free-willing community. Though nearly wiped out during the Thirty Years' War, they survived, and later their descendants, known as the Hutterites, immigrated to the United States. My own wife and children are proud descendants of these brave farmers who five centuries ago risked torture and death to live out a voluntary Christian vision of liberty, equality, and fraternity.

This issue of *Plough* springs from a core Radical Reformation conviction: that there is a common life that overcomes economic exploitation, a life that is both thoroughly practical and independent of the state. This alternative society is possible here and now; anyone can pursue it. What's more, it is a vision that has existed since Christianity's beginnings. It's at the heart of Jesus' Sermon on the Mount and throughout the New Testament, as well as in the writings of the Old Testament prophets. This vision is exemplified by the communal life of the first church in Jerusalem, in which "all who believed were together and had all things in common; they would sell their possessions and goods and distribute the proceeds to all, as any had need" (Acts 2:44–45).

Some long-time *Plough* readers are no doubt already muttering: here we go again. Yes we do, because the challenges posed by socialists touch on a part of Jesus' proclamation that mainstream Christianity has gone to almost comical lengths to avoid. Like Jesus' hard sayings on divorce or nonviolence, his teachings on riches and private property are politely sidelined, explained away as historically specific or as rhetorical exaggerations. Alternatively, these teachings are treated as a special vocation for monastics, mendicants, and missionaries, a heroic feat that the rank-and-file should not attempt. In the place of voluntary poverty and sacrificial generosity are substituted the middle-class virtues of stewardship and philanthropy.

Yet Jesus' economic teachings are just as integral to the life he taught as any of his other basic commands: love to neighbors and enemies, hatred of hypocrisy, truthfulness, sexual purity, or the works of mercy. These teachings are not free-floating maxims but are all intimately interrelated; the way of life outlined in the Sermon on the Mount is a single whole that at once enables and requires freedom from private possessions. "You cannot serve God and mammon" is a truth that cuts through all spheres of life, as Eberhard Arnold describes in this issue (page 39). The apostles and early church fathers reiterate the same bracing axiom.

This interrelationship cuts both ways: Christianity's loss of one element – its original economic radicalism – ends up undermining its other claims too. The sanctity of life would be far easier to defend if Christians could point to their own churches as communities that gave generous economic and emotional support to new mothers and to the families of children with disabilities. Marriages would be more likely to endure without divorce if freed from the stress of economic insecurity. "Do not worry about tomorrow" appears to be foolish advice – unless a person has a church community that will step in when she loses her job or suffers a serious illness. Even Jesus' command of nonviolence becomes more understandable (though no less counterintuitive) if one no longer has to defend one's private property in order for one's family to

The Visible Communion of Saints

Peter Riedemann (1506–1556), an early Anabaptist leader, wrote the 1542 apologia excerpted here as a defense to Philip of Hesse, a prince who was holding him prisoner.

Community of goods applies to both spiritual and material gifts. All of God's gifts, not only the spiritual but also the temporal, have been given so that they not be kept but be shared with each other. Therefore, the communion of saints should be visible not only in spiritual but also in temporal things. Paul says one person should not have abundance while another suffers want; instead, there should be equality (2 Cor. 8:7–15). . . .

The Creation still testifies today that at the beginning God ordained that people should own nothing individually but should have all things in common with each other (Gen. 1:26–29). However, by taking what they should have left, and by leaving what they should have taken (Gen. 3:2–12), people have gained possession of things and have become more accustomed to accumulating things and hardened in doing so. Through such appropriating and collecting of created things, people have been led so far from God that they have forgotten the Creator (Rom. 1:18–25).

Source: *Peter Riedemann's Hutterite Confession of Faith*, trans. and ed. John J. Friesen (Plough, 2019), 119.

Community Is a Gift of the Spirit

From Foundations of Our Faith and Calling, *the Bruderhof's 2012 community rule.*

God wants to gather a people on earth who belong to his new creation. He calls them out to form a new society that makes his justice and peace tangible. Among them private property falls away, and they are united in a bond of solidarity and equality in which each one says: Whatever I have belongs to the others, and if I am ever in need, they will help me. Then Jesus' words can come true: "Do not be anxious, saying, 'What shall we eat?' or 'What shall we drink?' or 'What shall we wear?' For the Gentiles seek all these things; and your heavenly Father knows that you need them all. But seek first his kingdom and his righteousness, and all these things shall be yours as well" (Matt. 6:31–33).

Such a people came into being in Jerusalem at the first Pentecost. As described in Acts 2 and 4, the Holy Spirit descended on the believers who had gathered after Jesus' resurrection, and the first communal church was born. Just as it was then, so it will be today whenever the Spirit is poured out on a group of people. They will be filled with love for Christ and for one another, and their communion of love will lead them to share their goods, talents, and lives, boldly testifying to the gospel. This is our calling in church community.

Source: *Foundations of Our Faith and Calling* (Plough, 2012), 5.

survive. These are just a few examples of the convincing power that Christianity would gain by refusing to compromise with mammon.

Christian cultural leaders, including those who cultivate a radical brand, don't shy from provocation when it comes to morality, politics, or theology – but they tend to tread gingerly around the dollars and cents of discipleship. Again and again one meets the same bald assertion that a life of economic sharing is marginal, sectarian, literalistic, extremist, and just not doable.

It's important to make a distinction that the New Testament doesn't speak of voluntary poverty and community of goods as rigid ethical demands, as if owning property were a sin in itself such as lust or idolatry. This misunderstanding stems from the legalistic need to reduce discipleship to a list of duties and prohibitions. Far from it: community of goods in the New Testament is simply the practical expression of love when it overflows into economics. Naturally, this can take many different forms. Here's some first-hand evidence that a life beyond capitalism is not as unattainable as it's made out to be:

This summer the Bruderhof community celebrates the beginning of its hundredth year of living together in full community of goods. Over its history, our community has had its share of imperfections and follies, just like any group of human beings. But by the grace of God, and with thanks to friends far and near, we're still here.

The Bruderhof originated in an unusually fertile and febrile moment: Germany immediately after World War I. In 1920 the theologian Eberhard Arnold moved with his family from Berlin to a small village to start an intentional community. Initially, this was a circle of young Christians disillusioned with the church's complicity in the militarism that led to World War I. With the Sermon on the Mount as their charter, they drew inspiration from the early church and the Anabaptists as well as Francis and Clare of Assisi, the early Quakers, and the religious socialist movement that included Christoph Blumhardt and Karl Barth. The idea of a rural settlement came from Gustav Landauer, a Jewish anarchist visionary who had been assassinated by right-wing thugs the previous year (page 112); Landauer also inspired the kibbutz movement, which was forming around the same time.

> ## "We do not speak great things, we live them."
> *Minucius Felix*

A century later, our community remains small in comparison with many churches. Still, it's home to three thousand people of many nationalities – in two dozen locations on five continents – who live together and share everything. In our case, this sharing takes the form of a lifelong vow of poverty: we each own literally nothing.

My point in mentioning these details is not self-congratulation but simply to establish an empirical fact: it is possible for people to live this way. It's possible in diverse geographic settings, with significant cultural variety, over five or six generations.

And of course the Bruderhof is just one recent example in the long history of Christian community. "See how they love one another," the pagans exclaimed about the early church according to Tertullian in AD 197. The love that impressed the pagans wasn't a matter of tender feelings but of concrete acts of mutual help, as the historian Alan Kreider describes in his book *The Patient Ferment of the Early Church*. In the words of the third-century Christian lawyer Minucius Felix, "We do not speak great things, we live them." The Christians formed an alternative society in which the educated and illiterate, slave and free, served each other as brothers and sisters, with none calling anything their own if another had greater need. To use Wordsworth's phrase, they were the "strong in love."

Starting with the early church and then the birth of monasticism in the Egyptian desert, this history includes groups as diverse as 1500-year-old Benedictine orders, reformist movements like the Franciscans, the Waldensians of the medieval period, the Beguines and Beghards, the Moravian Brethren, the Jesuit *reducciones* in Paraguay and Brazil, the Little Gidding community immortalized by T. S. Eliot, the Jesus Family in China, Dorothy Day's Catholic Worker movement, and Latin America's *comunidades del base*. Numerous communities across the denominational spectrum exist today, from the Catholic Focolare communities based in Italy, to the Evangelical Adsideo community in Oregon, to the Anglican Jesus Abbey in South Korea.

This history should serve to remind us of the possibilities of the present. As a new generation asks hard questions about justice, solidarity, and human happiness, we Christians must remember that we have had access to the answers all along. Of all people we should know: another life is possible.

We don't need a shallow social justice Christianity that lurches from one progressive cause to the next. We can have the real thing: the way of life Jesus taught in the Sermon on the Mount. This life is there for the having. It is bliss to be alive. ⤜

Harro Preiss,
*Farmer Boy at
Oberfellendorf*

Artwork by Harro Preiss. Used by permission.

Thank you for your wonderful issue, *The Welcome Table* (Spring 2019), which seemed like a virtual Babette's feast! I was somewhat uncomfortable, however, with what seemed like an unquestioning view of meat consumption. While I am not a vegetarian or vegan, I am increasing aware of the building evidence that worldwide meat consumption, especially beef consumption, is probably the leading cause of greenhouse gas emissions today. The ongoing destruction of forests to raise more beef and the increasing production of methane from beef is a serious problem. Perhaps inviting a vegetarian or vegan to the Welcome Table to share their commitments might have made the meal more complete. In the end, questions regarding how we can best care for creation are complex, and I applaud the efforts of the farmers and ranchers whose stories are found in the spring *Plough Quarterly.*   Steve Bisset, Naples, NY

I wanted to write a quick note of thanks for the work you are doing with *Plough Quarterly.* I have received complimentary copies of the magazine for the past several issues and your magazine has become one of my favorite reads. In fact, I plan to subscribe later tonight to show my appreciation! Yours is one of the few magazines that brings me joy as I read each issue. This past issue on food and hospitality was excellent. Blessings in your continued good work.

Jacob Walsh, Vice President and Publisher,
Christianity Today

On Johannes Meier's interview "Beating the Big Dry" (Spring 2019): I painted "Farmer Boy at Oberfellendorf" in response to the photograph of young people planting olive trees in Australia. *(See above.)*

Harro Preiss, Germany

As usual, I read *The Welcome Table* (spring 2019 issue) with interest. As I set down this issue, however, it seemed that something was missing from the discussion. There was nothing about the importance of family meals. Eating together as a family not only strengthens the bonds between parents and children, but it creates an event, a gathering to which others can be invited. At family meals, the practice of thinking of others, welcoming and serving them, and enjoying the company of friends from beyond the family circle can be instilled in children. Learning to welcome those who may seem strange, or difficult to be with, those who are lonely and without their own families, or visitors who show up unannounced, are important values for parents to teach young children.

Judith Shirky, Esopus, NY

We welcome letters to the editor. Letters and web comments may be edited for length and clarity, and may be published in any medium. Letters should be sent with the writer's name and address to letters@plough.com. ➤

Family & Friends AROUND THE WORLD

Image courtesy of Stephen Addison

Is Faith a Force for Good in the Family?

In theory, advocating for strong families should be boringly uncontroversial. After all, most people agree that children deserve to grow up in stable homes in which parents have the time and resources to be good fathers and mothers. In reality, though, family policy is deeply polarizing. That's tragic, because the stakes are high, especially for disadvantaged children. Much needs to be done here, but one essential first step is good research and hard facts about what helps children, and what harms them.

That's the mission of the Institute for Family Studies (IFS) in Washington, DC. They've been praised by *New York Times* columnist Ross Douthat for "transforming the culture wars we have into the debates that we desperately need."

In May 2019, IFS published a rich, multifaceted report titled *The Ties that Bind: Is Faith a Global Force for Good or Ill in the Family?*. Based on an original survey of 16,474 people in the Americas, Europe, and Oceania, the report looks at the relationship between religion and four important outcomes in families: relationship quality, fertility, domestic violence, and infidelity. Overall, findings indicate that "the family-friendly norms and networks associated with religious communities reinforce the ties that bind; the challenge facing those communities, however, is to build on these strengths to address families who are struggling." In what has been called a post-familial age, this often eye-opening report deserves a wide readership. Read it at *ifstudies.org/the-ties-that-bind*.

Box Up Crime founder Stephen Addison with a student

Box Up Crime

Growing up in a deprived estate in East London, Stephen Addison felt he had no choice but to go into a life of crime. Like many adolescents, he found the pull of his peer group to be stronger than parental advice, and became involved with criminal activities at a young age. Stephen's life changed at the age of twenty when he became a Christian. He went to university and got a business degree but remained concerned about the almost inevitable involvement with gangs and crime for many young people growing up in his neighborhood. Stephen started the youth organization Box Up Crime to offer a way out. Based in the Barking and Dagenham borough of London, the organization goes into schools and community centers to give boxing training and mentoring to young people. They now work with up to six hundred youths each week and are expanding. There has been a 25 percent drop in crime in the areas in which they work, and more importantly, they are providing hope and encouragement to young people who badly need it. Stephen's message to

Image courtesy of Joy Kauffman

Joseph Malish teaching FARM STEW's food pyramid to refugees during a training.

young people is, "You need to find a positive alternative." Box Up Crime is there to provide one. *boxupcrime.org*

Soymilk versus Civil War

Joy Kauffman

Joseph Malish is a church elder, a trainer, and one of a million refugees from South Sudan living in Uganda. He has another name, too: "Malish Leben." His new name means milk, and in a country with one of the world's worst refugee crises, it represents hope for peace.

Malish's mission is to teach refugees how to transform soybeans into milk. It's his response to the violence among the country's tribes, often triggered by disputes over access to pastureland and water for their dairy cattle. Ethnic militias sweep down on unprotected villages, killing people and stealing livestock. Joseph Malish believes soymilk could help end

fighting that has caused thousands of deaths and driven millions from their homes.

Malish is one of twenty-five African trainers in the FARM STEW organization, founded with the hope of equipping vulnerable families with skills to prevent hunger, disease, and poverty. FARM STEW is an acronym, standing for eight ingredients required for abundant living: Farming, Attitude, Rest, Meals, Sanitation, Temperance, Enterprise, and Water. In early 2019, FARM STEW launched a new team in South Sudan at the invitation of local churches.

In FARM STEW trainings, as many as forty-two tribes come together, including Nuer and Dinka, two tribes that both prize cattle and milk highly and so have become bitter enemies. At a recent training, Malish (who is multilingual) asked a Nuer to translate for a Dinka. During the eight-hour training, the group worked together preparing local foods. At the end of class, they sat together eating from common pots and drinking soymilk. Many participants said they wanted to come back for more. Joseph Malish predicts that the capacity of refugees to make their own milk could be a key to healing for his nation. Learn more at *farmstew.org.*

Joy Kauffman, MPH, is a nutritionist who served with the USAID Farmer to Farmer program in Uganda and is the founder and president of FARM STEW. farmstew.org

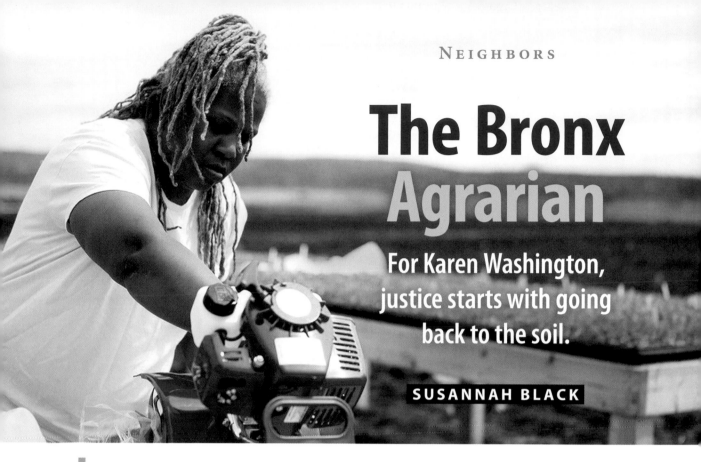

The Bronx Agrarian

For Karen Washington, justice starts with going back to the soil.

SUSANNAH BLACK

In 1985, when Karen Washington began gardening in the back yard of her small house in the Bronx, there were four things she wanted to grow. Collard greens, she says, "because that has been a staple in the African American community and culture." Eggplant "sounded funky and different." Peppers, "because I liked peppers, and then I wanted to grow a tomato, because I hated tomatoes."

The tomatoes were what changed her world. The taste was nothing like the grocery store tomatoes of her childhood.

Washington, a physical therapist, did not come from any kind of farming background; nor had her parents nor grandparents. She was born and raised on New York's Lower East Side, and then moved with her parents and brother to Harlem.

But in 1985, when she was thirty-one, she moved uptown to the Bronx. Several years later,

to reclaim vacant lots and encourage middle-class settlement, borough president Fernando Ferrer started giving tax breaks to developers to build single-family homes – homes with a bit of land attached.

She jumped at the chance. "I decided that I wanted to grow food, and so I had to go to the library, I had to buy books, and then speak to some people."

When the development project foundered for lack of money, vacant lots were left, including one right across the street from the house in which Washington and her family were now living. "I know what it means to live across from a vacant lot," she says, "they become full of garbage, and then I know what people say about you living in areas where there's garbage." Washington was not going to let that vacant lot sit there. She turned it into her first community garden.

Karen Washington servicing a tiller at Rise & Root Farm in Chester, New York

Susannah Black is a contributing editor to Plough *and has written for publications including* First Things, Mere Orthodoxy, *and* The American Conservative. *She lives in New York City.*

Before 1998, things went smoothly. Washington explains, "People took these community gardens and turned them into oases, so that beauty and hope, strength and resilience was brought back to communities that for so long had been suffering . . . from these garbage-filled lots."

But then things changed. "I got scars," she says. As land values increased, the city started to see the community gardens as potential developable property. In the middle of one night in 1998, Mayor Rudolph Giuliani tried to auction off one hundred community gardens. It felt like a betrayal, and a huge blow to the movement. But in retrospect, Washington says it was the best thing that could have happened, because people woke up to their need to fight for the gardens. Washington had never really been political, and she hadn't thought of gardening as being political. But she realized that growing food in a city does have political consequences. The gardeners pushed back. They gathered allies: churches, restaurants, people from all five boroughs. "You're told you can't fight city hall," she says, "but yes, we did. We fought city hall."

> **I wanted to grow a tomato, because I hated tomatoes.**

Eliot Spitzer, the attorney general at the time, paid attention, issuing an injunction against the bulldozing of the gardens, and the land was officially ceded to various public trust and private nongovernmental organizations.

The experience gave Washington a realistic sense of what it takes to garden in cities. "It's always about development," she says, "and we have to have a say in how that development looks, we have to make sure that within cities, there is green space, that we're not surrounded by concrete jungles."

So she's continuing to garden, but she's also continuing to organize. Every time there is a new administration up for election in New York, she has a candidates' forum, letting the hopefuls know that if they want a shot at office, they have to protect the community gardens.

What started as a few neighbors banding together is now part of the urban agriculture movement. And that movement is not small. "That's primarily because in low-income neighborhoods, and especially neighborhoods of color," says Washington, "we don't have local healthy food options. . . . It's not rocket science: when you're living in an area where you don't have access to healthy food, and you don't have access to culturally appropriate food, people will do something about that."

Food justice, she is convinced, is part of racial justice. In 2010, she and some friends started the first Black Farmers and Urban Gardeners' Conference, now called Black Urban Growers (BUGS). At the farms and conferences she visited to discuss food justice and sustainability, she didn't see people like herself. "And I could feel my ancestors just saying, 'Karen, you know, don't forget who we are.' For so long, African Americans have been leaving the land, and . . . we're getting all kinds of diet-related diseases. Now you see so many young black men and women who want to farm; there's a rebirth of knowledge about who we are as African Americans and as agrarians."

But relearning that connection, and learning to trust it, is not always easy. Washington recalls an organic growing program at the Center for Agroecology and Sustainable Food Systems, in 2008, which included training on a nine-acre farm: "The first day that I went out to the field, I didn't want to go. I was fearful." She hadn't realized what it would be like, in a sense, to go back: it was as field hands that so many of her ancestors had been enslaved, and she could still feel that oppression and trauma. Yet, reconnecting to the land itself was what healed:

I literally went to the soil and put both my hands in that soil, and I felt that belonging, and I'll never forget that, because now I understand my true connection to the land. At the end of the day, we come from the soil, we're going to go back to the soil. Understanding that gave me a sense of power.

Six years later, in 2014, she retired from physical therapy, and with several friends, formed Rise & Root Farm on three acres in Chester, New York. The farm is organized as a cooperative, with all decisions made collectively. Their land abuts several other farms, all of which abide by a general common vision. "We share infrastructure, ideas, and tools," she says, "and follow the mission of food justice and social justice."

Washington sees the land as a trust from God, and the story of her own Christian faith is intimately tied to her work. "I grew up Catholic," she says, "and then I went away from the church for a long time, and didn't find a direction." But then she started working with Father John C. Flynn. As well as a priest, he was something else that she recognized: a community organizer. They were both part of a neighborhood group called the Northwest Bronx Community & Clergy Coalition. "He was a guy who would walk the streets reaching out to youth who were lost in their way. . . . He was some man."

At a protest in Washington, DC, with Father Flynn, Washington copped to him that she didn't go to church. "Karen, the church isn't a building," he said to her.

"No one ever spoke to me like that. And I said 'You know what? You're the priest who goes from the pews to the streets, and I'm going to meet you half way, I'm gonna come from the street to the pews.'" So she did. For the past fifteen years Washington has been a parishioner at St. Martin of Tours, where

Father Flynn was pastor before his death in 2012. She's also a lay Eucharistic minister.

St. Martin of Tours is just a few blocks away from her house, and from her first vacant-lot-turned-community garden. "When you think about these vacant lots," she says, "you have to think of the word community." But the work of creating community does not stop at gardening. Washington tells a story about one of the many recent Mexican immigrants in the neighborhood. The woman had a tumor growing on her neck, which she covered self-consciously. Yet she gradually began to drop the covering as she felt more and more at home among the gardeners. "And so, what we did, as a garden," Washington recalls, "we reached out to our community people . . . because she didn't have any insurance, she was undocumented, and we found a doctor who was able to perform surgery to remove the growth, for free. The community put their arms around her, with that deformity she had, and then here was a group of people who gathered together to work behind the scenes. This is what community is."

Washington now splits her time between her community in the Bronx and the farm in Chester. Her children are grown and thriving, and she has two grandsons. "I'll be sixty-five this year," she says, "and I want to be able to say, at the end of my time, that I made a difference in someone's life, that God is proud of me. I never, never take my life for granted. Whatever I get, I share with people. We have one life to live." ⟩⟩

The McDonald's Test

Learning to Love
Back Row America

AN INTERVIEW WITH CHRIS ARNADE

Once a Wall Street banker, Chris Arnade spent three years crisscrossing the United States to visit "the places you were told not to go to." His travels took him from the Bronx to the Ozarks to East Los Angeles. He shares what he learned in *Dignity*, **a searing new book of essays and photojournalism.** *Plough*'s **Peter Mommsen caught up with him to talk about fast-food joints, storefront churches, meritocracy, and whether to give cash to panhandlers.**

Plough: **What pushed you into starting this hugely time-consuming project?**

Chris Arnade: It started in 2012 when I was a bond trader for a prestigious Wall Street bank. I'd been doing that for twenty years, and wanted to see more of the world. So I started taking long walks through New York City. And soon, I found myself going to places that people in my social group told me not to go to.

One of those was Hunts Point, a neighborhood in the South Bronx that has a reputation as a center for drugs and prostitution. I ended up spending three years there. I became very close to homeless people, sex workers, addicts – some whose stories appear in the book. It was simply my attempt to listen to people no one else would listen to.

In 2015, I decided to branch out to other places across the United States that are disregarded or talked negatively about. Places like Lewiston, Maine, or Bakersfield, California, or El Paso, Texas.

In that time, you covered over 150,000 miles. What motivation kept you going?

One motivation was political: a sense of outrage. When you're born into Hunts Point you have a lot working against you.

Previous spread: High school soccer team in Lewiston, Maine, which has a large Somali American community *(left)*; bingo day in a McDonald's in Louisiana *(right)*

It seems like our entire legal, economic, and cultural system is rigged against these kids. Yet they are no different than individuals you will find in the Upper East Side – they're not dumber, they're not any less hard-working. Here I was, someone who had lived in New York for twenty years in a comfortable life, counting myself a liberal, in this town where there is awful poverty and injustice. I wanted to find out if the same was true elsewhere.

The second motivation was personal. The first year or two that I was working on this project was surreal, since I was still working on Wall Street. Weekends or evenings I would go into "rough" neighborhoods with my camera and talk to people. Ultimately I chose to leave my job and do what I'm doing because I was – I am – happier. It's a very selfish reason. But I was more comfortable around the people in Hunts Point than I was with people on Wall Street.

When you visited one crumbling Missouri town, the locals greeted you with the words, "You must be here to write about crystal meth." How does a book about poor communities avoid voyeurism?

The phrase people use for it is "poverty porn." My comeback is, "I think we need a little more poverty porn. We have enough luxury porn."

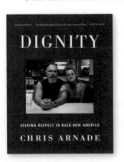

Chris Arnade grew up in Florida, got a PhD in physics from Johns Hopkins University, and worked with a Wall Street bank before becoming a freelance writer and photographer. His work has appeared in the New York Times, *the* Atlantic, *the* Guardian, *and the* Financial Times. *His new book* Dignity: Seeking Respect in Back Row America *was published by Sentinel in June 2019.*

Of course, there is a bad way to write about people in these communities. I think it's entirely about methodology and intent. I go into communities sometimes without reading anything beforehand, so as not to bring along preconceived notions.

One place I visited was Prestonsburg, Kentucky. The center of that community is a plaza with a McDonald's and a Walmart. Each day I was there, I saw a gentleman smoking cigarettes on a picnic table outside; he worked a night shift at one of the stores. Each day he'd refuse to talk. After twelve days, he said, "All right, you can take my picture." We chatted, and he gave me some quotes, and we laughed. At the end, he said, "Don't just tell the story about how Prestonsburg is filled with drugs and addicts. I hope you tell the story about how we're good people, too."

That is my intention with this book. Across all the communities I visited, which were so different, I found that same desire for dignity.

Along the way, you visited eight hundred McDonald's restaurants. Why?

My old self, my successful bond-trader self, used to look at McDonald's as an embarrassing place that I'd never go to. But when I started visiting Hunts Point, I found myself eating at McDonald's all the time. It was one of the few public places in the community that worked.

I became close friends with some homeless heroin addicts, and their life in many ways revolved around McDonald's. It's where they go to the bathroom to clean up. It's where they can plug in their phone and charge it. It's where they can just sit quietly for an hour and not be bothered, to escape the heat or cold. It's also where they get cheap food. I may not ethically respect the food, but it's cheap and it tastes good. For people who don't have much money, that counts for a lot. There was a real sense of community there.

I began to see that all across the country, the McDonald's restaurants were in fact

A McDonald's customer in Indiana

community centers. In towns where things are really dysfunctional, where government services are failing and non-profits and the private sector are failing to help people, McDonald's is one of the few places that still is open, still has a functional bathroom, and the lights are on.

Eventually I came up with what I call the McDonald's test. The broad thesis of my book is that our society sorts people into what I call the front row and the back row – the privileged class to which I used to belong, who are financially secure and live in safe neighborhoods with good schools and public services – and everybody else. The test is to ask a person: how do you view McDonald's? In my experience, the answer usually reveals whether someone belongs to the front or back row.

I understand the anti-McDonald's sentiment – what these vast global corporations have done in this intensely competitive, intensely materialistic world. What these companies care about is coming into a neighborhood, making money, and taking it out, and of course McDonald's is also guilty of this.

But the reality is that McDonald's is important in poor people's lives. People really want a sense of community – they crave the social so much that they'll form communities in places that are meant to be entirely transactional. McDonald's, of course, is designed to get you in and get you out as quickly as possible. But what I found were old men's groups, old women's groups, Bible studies, chess games.

You also visited many churches. As an atheist, what was that like?

I was certainly an atheist when I began; it's more complicated now. Initially, I went to church for the same reason I was going to McDonald's: it was where the people I was speaking to were going. I didn't discriminate,

Milwaukee,
Wisconsin

I just went to whatever church or mosque was there, whatever faith was reflective of the community.

Like McDonald's, the churches worked. They were often the only institutions that were lit up and functional; usually they were storefront operations. You'd go down a street that was boarded up, derelict buildings, and then there was a church. Its doors weren't closed.

There aren't many success stories in my book – there's almost nobody who got out of a negative lifestyle. The only people who succeeded did it through faith – through the church. And so I had at first a grudging respect, and then a full-blown respect for what churches are doing.

Many of the people you met who lead lifestyles at odds with traditional faith – a transsexual prostitute, for example – still put the Bible at the center of their lives.

You go into a crack house, you'll find a Bible or a Quran. There will be all sorts of crazy things going on, but they'll be religious. Part of that's outreach; the religious community does a wonderful job of serving the poor. But also, they find within the Bible, and within churches, a community that gets them. Yes, there are strains that judge them, but most of these churches don't ask much. They say, "Try to live this lifestyle and we'll accept you."

I also think that what they see in the Bible is an acceptance of failure, or at least the

recognition that everybody's a sinner and that we're all fallen and that we don't really have this all figured out. And that there is something out there greater than us. If you're living in a crack house and you see the vast injustices of this world at a visceral level, the idea that this is all that exists isn't appealing at all.

People like myself – wealthy, educated, scientific – have removed ourselves from the evidence of faith. I think it's much easier to see the Bible as something important if you're living on the streets and you understand mortality, you understand failure, you understand humility.

How did your travels change your views on success and meritocracy?

We've decided to sort ourselves by education – the idea is that being educated is the most important thing in life and that if you fail at that, it's your fault. Even in polite company, one can make fun of someone for not doing well at school. It's not just that we have a system that rewards education, it's that we have a very narrow definition of what being smart is.

This mindset is deeply materialistic, and it depends on an idolization of credentials, usually a university degree. Success is then defined by how much money you make and how many credentials you collect.

The problem with defining success like this is that, though it's easy to measure how much education or money someone has, it's

Shopping plaza in rural Kentucky

very hard to measure the value of being a good parent or of deciding to stay in your hometown and to spend your life contributing to it. With a meritocratic mindset, when we fail to find things we can put numbers on, we tend to overlook their value.

What do the alternative kinds of success look like?

When I was spending time in East Los Angeles, which is largely a Mexican American neighborhood, there was a McDonald's I used to go to in order to write up my notes. I noticed a young woman in there every night. I asked, "Why are you here every night?" She said, "I need the Wi-Fi. We don't have money for it in our home." She was going to a community college nearby.

When she found out I was from New York, she told me she'd love to go to school there. I offered to put her in touch with good schools, but she said she couldn't. It turned out she was the oldest daughter of a family of six, and she was the translator for the family.

By the usual standards of success, she was foolish for turning down the opportunity. But I don't know if that's right. She wanted to be there for her family.

In Reno, Nevada, I met an African American teenager who had turned down a chance to go to an out-of-state university and went to a local community college instead. His main reason was that his mom was sober after being an addict for twelve years, and he needed to be there for her.

I happen to think those two children made the right decision. If you had told me this story ten years ago, I'm not sure I would've thought so. There's a sense that we're all supposed to be independent franchises that just move wherever we want. There's no sense of place.

What lesson was hardest for you to learn?

When I started out on this project, I wanted to help the drug dealers and sex workers in Hunts Point. After a couple of years, I realized that I didn't understand the realities of the people I claimed I was helping.

I learned that the reality of the educated elite is just so different than the reality of the working class. It goes from what you think to what you eat to where you shop to who you interact with. That removal, that separation means, over time, you still don't understand each other. The educated elite don't understand the working class and vice versa. It goes both ways, but it's the educated elite who have removed themselves.

Take Walmart. There are a lot of reasons not to like Walmart, but if you want to get to know the immigrant community in a town, start with Walmart. Of course, many middle-class people do go to Walmart, but they generally don't go at two in the morning, which is when it can be most interesting. A lot of Walmarts have this wonderful policy where they let people park overnight, so people who are homeless will sleep in their cars in Walmart plazas, and then use the Walmart bathrooms in the morning. I found these stores to be one of the best places to interact with people who are often invisible.

Educated people, what I call the front row, don't understand such details of life. But they also don't understand the way people in the back row think, what they emphasize – which is often family, place, and faith, not career and credentials.

I'm afraid that the gap is now so large that we speak two different languages. It took me a while to be able to translate between the two.

Immigration has become a political rallying cry in most Western countries. Critics of immigration claim that it dilutes cultural

identity and so weakens community, especially in working-class areas. Did you find that to be the case?

Nothing could be more wrong than that statement. Often, the only thing that's working in these towns is the immigrant community. Lewiston, Maine, was all white and Christian up until 1998 – now it's 15 percent black and Muslim after the arrival of Somali immigrants. They've taken an empty, abandoned downtown and turned it into a vibrant part of town.

For me as a Southerner who has spent the past decades in New York, it was often a shock to visit small southern towns and find a thriving Mexican American community. Often they're the only ones running family-owned restaurants and businesses in neighborhoods that had emptied out.

You can't deny, though, that the speed of change in these towns is scary to many old-timers. Communities that have had a strong sense of local identity for two hundred years are suddenly turned on their heads. Many of these communities have suffered a lot, and immigrants can become an easy scapegoat.

For example, in Lewiston I met a working-class white guy, a Vietnam veteran. Things haven't been going well for him for thirty years; he lives off and on in Section 8 housing; he's in and out of addiction. Every week, when he goes to get his food distribution, he has to wait in line – and in recent years he's had to wait longer, because half the people in front of him are Somalis. I won't repeat the words he said. They were not pleasant, but it's easy to see how he got there. Immigration, to him, is easy to blame.

You suggest that one thing which may have stayed more the same than people would like to admit is racism.

There's awful racism in the United States, which cannot be denied or diminished. What's forgotten, though, is that the most progressive towns are often the most segregated. We tend to focus on the ugly incidents of racism that happen among the white working class and ignore the racism of the elites, which is less overt because it's structural. It's a matter of zoning laws, of where the best schools are, who is more likely to be arrested or imprisoned, where good jobs are available.

Three hundred yards from the US–Mexico border in El Paso, Texas

Day laborer in Selma, Alabama

My visit to Milwaukee, which is well-known for its progressive politics, illustrated this to me. Historically, the African American community was intentionally confined to a tiny neighborhood in the city, and it's largely still concentrated there. Most African Americans came there in the 1940s and 50s from the same part of Mississippi. I spent a lot of time with the older members of this community, who had grown up in the segregated South and then moved north. They repeatedly told me, "The racism here isn't any better than it was there." Milwaukee was already electing socialists to the US Congress a century ago. But these men told me, "Look, the racism is different here. The racism in the South was in your face. Here, it's behind your back – they talk the talk but don't walk the walk." In their eyes, they were still confined to the secondary jobs and to a secondary neighborhood, with high barriers keeping the young people in their place.

One of the most haunting sections in your book describes Selma, Alabama, which is best known for its role in the civil rights movement. You write how you found beautifully kept historic monuments to the Selma Marches of 1964 surrounded by crumbling housing projects.

I love Selma – people were very warm to me there. But they aren't happy. There are nice parts of Selma, but they're small and contained. The reality for most people there, for most African Americans, is disenfranchisement, not only legal but economic. In all the places I visited, I never saw people carrying firearms or dealing drugs so openly and nonchalantly as in Selma.

There's an anger, a justified anger, among the people there, and a quiet bitterness and cynicism about whether political action can fix anything. (Of course, Alabama has made it very easy for blacks not to vote – in fact, they've done everything they can to make them not vote.) The reality of Selma today suggests that the civil rights victories of the 1960s were largely symbolic. Far more needs to be done.

You said earlier that at first you wanted to help people, then learned you had to understand them first. But how do you help someone who seems trapped in a negative pattern?

I think the best thing you can do is provide moments of dignity – listen to them, treat them like a normal person. If someone needs a clean meal, give them a clean meal; if someone needs to go to the hospital, take them.

I often get asked by people, "Well, there's a homeless person near me. What should I do?" Just treat him or her like a normal person. Sit down and talk. Invite them for coffee, genuinely. If you have shared interests, explore them. Don't be fake friendly.

One of the things I learned to do is hug everybody. I don't care how dirty they are – I've hugged people who haven't bathed in two or three months. It's a sign that you're willing to treat them like a normal person. You should treat everybody with dignity, but in particular for people who are on the cusp, it's the one thing that may matter most.

Does that include giving money to panhandlers?

Yes. I always keep a five-dollar bill in my pocket – people who beg often look at me funny because I'll take out one thousand dollars from my wallet, all in fives. Most drugs cost nine dollars, so I give less than that. If I hand somebody five dollars and they ask for four dollars more, I know exactly what's going on. I may invite them to McDonald's and buy them a meal.

What do you hope people will do after reading your book?

Look at what's of value beyond material things. Many people are mad about the world, but there's actually never been a better time to craft a life beyond capitalism than there is now.

In Hunts Point, I got to know an addict – her name was Millie. She died. I only know this because she went missing and I spent a bunch of weeks tracking her down. In New York City, if you die without paperwork or identification, you get sent to Hart Island, where a million bodies are buried. You're put in a plywood box, put into a trench, and buried by inmates from Rikers Island. People generally aren't allowed to visit the grave.

When I finally learned that Millie was dead and where she was buried, it started me thinking. There's a saying: "You don't really die until people stop talking about you." If that's true, if you're buried on Hart Island in a plywood box with no way to visit, you're going to die much quicker. Your memory's just going to disappear.

So I ended up helping get Millie's body exhumed and properly buried. I went into it thinking, "As an atheist, why am I doing this? Who cares where you're buried? You're dead." But this symbolic action mattered immensely to Millie's street family. There was a memorial you could visit. There was a gravestone. Her memory was going to stay on a little bit more.

So don't fetishize poverty. But be a little bit more willing to go into the neighborhood people told you not to go into. Take time to listen to people. Give them respect. ➤

Interview by Peter Mommsen on April 30, 2019.

"Do not lay up for yourselves treasures on earth, where moth and rust consume and where thieves break in and steal, but lay up for yourselves treasures in heaven, where neither moth nor rust consumes and where thieves do not break in and steal. For where your treasure is, there will your heart be also.

"No one can serve two masters; for either he will hate the one and love the other, or he will be devoted to the one and despise the other. You cannot serve God and mammon.

"Therefore I tell you, do not be anxious about your life, what you shall eat or what you shall drink, nor about your body, what you shall put on. Is not life more than food, and the body more than clothing? Look at the birds of the air: they neither sow nor reap nor gather into barns, and yet your heavenly Father feeds them. Are you not of more value than they? . . .

"Therefore do not be anxious, saying, "What shall we eat?" or "What shall we drink?" or "What shall we wear?" For the Gentiles seek all these things; and your heavenly Father knows that you need them all. But seek first his kingdom and his righteousness, and all these things shall be yours as well." —*Jesus of Nazareth*

Matthew 6:19–21, 24–33

"They devoted themselves to the apostles' teaching and fellowship, to the breaking of bread and the prayers. And fear came upon every soul; and many wonders and signs were done through the apostles. And all who believed were together and had all things in common; and they sold their possessions and goods and distributed them to all, as any had need. And day by day, attending the temple together and breaking bread in their homes, they partook of food with glad and generous hearts, praising God and having favor with all the people. And the Lord added to their number day by day those who were being saved.

"Now the company of those who believed were of one heart and soul, and no one said that any of the things which he possessed was his own, but they had everything in common. And with great power the apostles gave their testimony to the resurrection of the Lord Jesus, and great grace was upon them all. There was not a needy person among them, for as many as were possessors of lands or houses sold them, and brought the proceeds of what was sold and laid it at the apostles' feet; and distribution was made to each as any had need." —*Luke the Evangelist*

Acts 2:42–47; 4:32–35

What Lies Beyond Capitalism?

A Christian Exploration

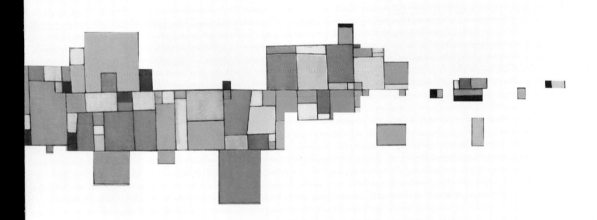

DAVID BENTLEY HART

Capitalism can't be reconciled with the teachings of Jesus of Nazareth – or so claims the New Testament translator David Bentley Hart. Christ condemned not just greed for riches, but their very possession, and Jesus' first followers were voluntary communists. With technologized market forces dominating our world, is a truly Christian economics still possible? What, if anything, lies beyond capitalism?

I : What Is Capitalism?

> Commerce is, in its essence, *satanic*.
> Commerce is the repayment of what was
> loaned, it is the loan made with the stipu-
> lation: Pay me more than I give you.
>
> —Baudelaire, *Mon cœur mis à nu*

I have no entirely satisfactory answer to the questions that prompt these reflections; but I do think the right *approach* to the answers can be glimpsed fairly clearly if we first take the time to define our terms. These days, after all, especially in America, the word *capitalism* has become a ridiculously capacious portmanteau word for every imaginable form of economic exchange, no matter how primitive or rudimentary. I take it, however, that here we are employing it somewhat more precisely, to indicate an epoch in the history of market economies that commenced in earnest only a few centuries ago. *Capitalism*, as many historians define it, is the set of financial conventions that took shape in the age of industrialization and that gradually supplanted the mercantilism of the previous era. As Proudhon defined it in 1861, it is a system in which as a general rule those whose work creates profits neither own the means of production nor enjoy the fruits of their labor.

This form of commerce largely destroyed the contractual power of free skilled labor, killed off the artisanal guilds, and introduced instead a mass wage system that reduced labor to a negotiable commodity. In this way, it created a market for the exploitation of cheap and desperate laborers. It was also increasingly abetted by government policies that reduced the options of the disadvantaged to wage-slavery or total indigence (such as Britain's enclosures of the commons starting in the middle of the eighteenth century). All of this, moreover, necessarily entailed a shift in economic eminence from the merchant class – purveyors of goods contracted from and produced by independent labor, subsidiary estates, or small local markets – to capitalist investors who both produce and sell their goods. And this, in the fullness of time, evolved into a fully realized corporate system that transformed the joint-stock companies of early modern trade into engines for generating immense capital at the secondary level of financial speculation: a purely financial market where wealth is created for and enjoyed by those who toil not, neither do they spin, but who instead engage in an incessant circulation of investment and divestment, as a kind of game of chance.

For this reason, capitalism might be said to have achieved its most perfect expression in the rise of the commercial corporation with limited liability, an institution that allows the game to be played in abstraction even from whether the businesses invested in ultimately succeed or fail. (One can profit just

---

David Bentley Hart is a philosopher, writer, translator, and cultural commentator. His books include, most recently, The New Testament: A Translation, *and the upcoming* That All Shall Be Saved: Heaven, Hell, and Universal Salvation *(Yale University, 2019).*

as much from the destruction of livelihoods as from their creation.) Such a corporation is a truly insidious entity: *Before* the law, it enjoys the status of a legal person – a legal privilege formerly granted only to "corporate" associations recognized as providing public goods, such as universities or monasteries – but *under* the law it is required to behave as the most despicable person imaginable. Almost everywhere in the capitalist world (in America, for instance, since the 1919 decision in *Dodge v. Ford*), a corporation of this sort is required to seek no end other than maximum gains for its shareholders; it is forbidden to allow any other consideration – say, a calculation of what constitutes decent or indecent profits, the welfare of laborers, charitable causes that might divert profits, or what have you – to hinder it in this pursuit.

The corporation is thus morally bound to amorality. And this whole system, obviously, not only allows for, but positively depends upon, immense concentrations of private capital and dispositive discretion over its use as unencumbered by regulations as possible. It also allows for the exploitation of material and human resources on an unprecedentedly massive scale. And, inevitably, it eventuates in a culture of consumerism, because it must cultivate a social habit of consumption extravagantly in excess of mere natural need or even (arguably) natural want. It is not enough to satisfy natural desires; a capitalist culture must ceaselessly seek to fabricate new desires, through appeals to what 1 John calls "the lust of the eyes."

The very least that one must concede is that capitalism "works." That is, it produces enormous wealth, and adapts itself with remarkable plasticity to even the most abrupt changes of cultural and material circumstances. When it has faltered, here or there, it has evolved new

TELL ME, do you really seek riches and financial gain from the destitute? If this person had the resources to make you even wealthier, why did he come begging to your door? He came seeking an ally but found an enemy. He came seeking medicine, and stumbled onto poison. Though you have an obligation to remedy the poverty of someone like this, instead you increase the need, seeking a harvest from the desert.

Basil of Caesarea, "Against Those Who Lend at Interest"

mechanisms for preventing the same mistake from being made again. It does not bring about a just distribution of wealth, of course; nor could it. A capitalist society not only tolerates, but positively requires, the existence of a pauper class, not only as a reserve of labor value, but also because capitalism relies on a stable credit economy, and a credit economy requires a certain supply of perennial debtors whose poverty – through predatory lending and interest practices – can be converted into capital

Deborah Batt, *Urban Village*

Previous spread: Deborah Batt, *Rural Decay*

Deborah Batt,
Community

for their creditors. The perpetual insolvency of the working poor and lower-middle class is an inexhaustible font of profits for the institutions upon which the investment class depends.

One can also concede that, now and then, the immense returns reaped by the few *can* redound to the benefit of the many; but there is no fixed rule to that effect, and generally quite the opposite is the case. Capitalism can create and enrich or destroy and impoverish, as prudence warrants; it can encourage liberty and equity or abet tyranny and injustice, as necessity dictates. It has no natural attachment to the institutions of democratic or liberal freedom. It has no moral nature at all. It is a system that cannot be abused, but only practiced with greater or lesser efficiency. But, of course, viewed from any intelligible moral perspective, that which is beyond the distinction between good and evil is, in its essence, evil.

For all these reasons, it seems wise to me that we have elected to ask ourselves not what comes *after* capitalism, but rather what lies *beyond* it. As far as I can see, what comes *after* capitalism – that is, what follows from it in the natural course of things – is nothing. This is not because I believe that the triumph of the bourgeois corporatist market state constitutes the "end of history," the final rational result of some inexorable material dialectic. Much less do I imagine that the logic of capitalism has won the future and that its reign is destined to be perpetual. In fact, I suspect that it is, in the long run, an unsustainable system.

My conviction is based, rather, on a very simple calculus of the disproportion between infinite appetite and finite resources. Of its nature, capitalism is a monstrously metastasized psychosis, one that will ultimately, if left to itself, reduce the whole of the natural order to a desert: despoiled, ravaged, poisoned, profaned. The whole planet is already immersed in an atmosphere of microplastic particles, wrapped in a thickening shroud of carbon emissions, whelmed in floods of heavy metals and toxins. And I have no expectation that any contrary impulse – say, the instinct of survival, a sane ethical consequentialism, a solicitude for nature, a spontaneous reverence for the glory of creation – will significantly impede its advance toward that inevitable terminus.

Essentially, capitalism is the process of securing evanescent material advantages through the permanent destruction of its own material basis. It is a system of total consumption, not simply in the commercial sense, but in the sense also that its necessary logic is the purest nihilism, a commitment to the transformation of concrete material plenitude into immaterial absolute value. I expect, therefore, that – barring the appearance, at an oblique angle, of some adventitious, countervailing agency – capitalism will not have exhausted its intrinsic energies until it has exhausted the world itself. That would, in fact, mark its final triumph: the total rendition of the last intractable residues of the merely intrinsically good into the impalpable Pythagorean eternity of market value. And any force capable of interrupting this process would have to come from beyond.

II : Beyond Capitalism

We know that the Jews were prohibited from investigating the future. . . . This does not imply, however, that for the Jews the future turned into homogeneous, empty time. For every second of time was the strait gate through which Messiah might enter.

—Walter Benjamin, "Theses on the Concept of History"

The ultimate horizon of that "beyond," to be honest, is not difficult to imagine. It is more or less the same thing that all sane rational wills long for, almost as a kind of transcendental: history's sabbath, blissful anarchy, pure communism, a human and terrestrial reality where acquisitive desire can find nothing to fasten upon because nothing is withheld, and nothing delightful or useful is out of reach, and all things are shared by a community of rational love. Even the blithering neo-liberal naïf who believes in supply-side economics is, unbeknownst to himself, an anarcho-communist in his profoundest transcendental intentions; somewhere deep within him a little Pyotr Kropotkin sleeps and dreams of a world purged of greed and violence. Everyone longs for the terrestrial paradise, for Eden as the end of the story rather than as its irrecoverable beginning.

But Eden is not the dialectical issue of

history, the final fruit of an occult rationality working itself out in and through the apparent contradictions of finitude. It is *beyond* in every sense. It inhabits time only as an eschatological judgment upon the present, a constant anamnesis of the good order of creation that we have always already betrayed. We know it principally as condemnation, and only secondarily as a sustaining hope. And how to translate that judgment into an agency immanent to history, one sufficiently powerful to disrupt the rule of capital before nothing remains to be saved, is the great question of all political thought of any real substance in the modern world.

It is a question, moreover, that Christians cannot avoid. Admittedly, the social and institutional history of the church gives one little hope that very many Christians have ever been acutely conscious of this. But, whether or not they care to acknowledge the full implications of their faith, Christians are still obliged to affirm that this eschatological judgment has indeed already appeared within history, and in a very particular material, social, and political form. In many ways, John's Gospel is especially troubling as regards the sheer inescapable immediacy of God's verdict upon every worldly structure of sin. There eschatology becomes almost perfectly immanent. There Christ passes through history as a light that reveals all things for what they are; and it is our reaction to him – our ability or inability to recognize that light – that shows us ourselves. To have seen him is to have seen the Father, and so to reject him is to claim the devil as one's father instead. Our hearts are laid bare, the deepest decisions of our secret selves are brought out into the open, and we are exposed for what we are – what we have made ourselves.

But it is not only John's Gospel, really, that tells us as much. The grand eschatological allegory of Matthew 25, for instance, says it too. In John's Gospel, one's failure to recognize Christ as the true face of the Father, the one who comes from above, is one's damnation, here and now. In Matthew's, one's failure to recognize the face of Christ – and therefore the face of God – in the abject and oppressed, the suffering and disenfranchised, is the revelation that one has chosen hell as one's home. All our works, as Paul says, will be proved by fire; and those whose work fails the test can be saved only "as by fire." Nor does the New Testament leave us in any doubt regarding the *only* political and social practices that can pass through that trial without being wholly consumed.

Whatever else capitalism may be, it is first and foremost a system for producing as much *private* wealth as possible by squandering as much as possible of humanity's *common* inheritance of the goods of creation. But Christ condemned not only an unhealthy preoccupation with riches, but the getting and keeping of riches as such. The most obvious example of this, found in all three synoptic Gospels, is the story of the rich young ruler, and of Christ's remark about the camel and the needle's eye.

But one can look anywhere in the Gospels for confirmation. Christ clearly means what he says when quoting the prophet: he has been anointed by God's Spirit to preach good tidings *to the poor* (Luke 4:18). To the prosperous, the tidings he bears are decidedly grim: "Woe to you who are rich, for you are receiving your comfort in full; woe to you who are full fed, for you shall hunger; woe to you who are now laughing, for you shall mourn and weep" (Luke 6:24–25). As Abraham tells Dives in Hades, "You fully received your good things during your lifetime . . . so now you suffer" (Luke 16:25). Christ not only demands that we give freely to all who ask from us (Matt. 5:42), with such prodigality that one hand is ignorant of the other's largesse (Matt. 6:3); he explicitly

forbids storing up earthly wealth – not merely storing it up too obsessively – and allows instead only the hoarding of the treasures of heaven (Matt. 6:19–20). He tells *all* who would follow him to sell all their possessions and give the proceeds away as alms (Luke 12:33), and explicitly states that "every one of you who does not give up all that he himself possesses is incapable of being my disciple" (Luke 14:33). As Mary says, part of the saving promise of the gospel is that the Lord "has filled the hungry with good things and sent the rich away starving" (Luke 1:53). James, of course, says it most strikingly:

> Come now, you who are rich, weep, howling at the miseries coming upon you; your riches are corrupted and moths have consumed your clothes; your gold and silver have corroded, and their rust will be a witness against you and will consume your flesh like fire. You have stored up treasure in the Last Days! See, the wages you have given so late to the laborers who have harvested your fields cry aloud, and the cries of those who have harvested your fields have entered the ear of the Lord Sabaoth. You have lived in luxury, and lived upon the earth in self-indulgence. You have fattened your hearts on a day of slaughter. (James 5:1–6)

Simply said, the earliest Christians were communists (as Acts tells us of the church in Jerusalem, and as Paul's epistles occasionally reveal), not as an accident of history but as an imperative of the faith. In fact, in preparing my own recent translation of the New Testament, there were many times when I found it difficult not to render the word *koinonia* (and related terms) as something like *communism*. I was prevented from doing so not out of any doubt regarding the aptness of that word, but partly because I did not want accidentally to associate the practices of the early Christians with the centralized state "communisms" of the twentieth century, and partly because the word is not adequate to capture all the dimensions – moral, spiritual, material – of the Greek term as the Christians of the first century evidently employed it. There can simply be no question that absolutely central to the gospel they preached was the insistence that private wealth and even private property were alien to a life lived in the Body of Christ.

Well into the patristic age, the greatest theologians of the church were still conscious of this. And, of course, throughout Christian history the original provocation of the early church has persisted in isolated monastic communities and has occasionally erupted in local "purist" movements: Spiritual Franciscans, Russian Non-Possessors, the Catholic Worker Movement, the Bruderhof, and so on.

Small intentional communities committed to some form of Christian collectivism are all very well, of course. At present, they may be the only way in which any real communal practice of the *koinonia* of the early church is possible at all. But they can also be a tremendous distraction, especially if their isolation from and simultaneous dependency upon the larger political order is mistaken for a sufficient realization of the ideal Christian polity. Then whatever prophetic critique they might bring to bear upon their society is, in the minds of most believers, converted into a mere special vocation, both exemplary and precious – perhaps even a sanctifying priestly presence within the larger church – but still possible only for the very few, and certainly not a model of practical politics.

Therein lies the gravest danger, because the full *koinonia* of the Body of Christ is not an option to be set alongside other equally plausible alternatives. It is not a private ethos or an elective affinity. It is a call not to withdrawal, but to revolution. It truly enters history as a

YOU RICH, how far will you push your frenzied greed? Are you alone to dwell on the earth? . . . Earth at its beginning was for all in common, it was meant for rich and poor alike; what right do you have to monopolize the soil? Nature knows nothing of the rich; all are poor when she brings them forth. Clothing and gold and silver, food and drink and covering – we are born without them all; naked she receives her children into the tomb, and no one can enclose one's acres there.

Ambrose of Milan, "On Naboth"

final judgment that has nevertheless already been passed; it is inseparable from the extraordinary claim that Jesus is Lord over all things, that in the form of life he bequeathed to his followers the light of the kingdom has truly broken in upon this world, not as something that emerges over the course of a long

Deborah Batt,
Dwelling 10

IS NOT THE PERSON who strips another of clothing called a thief? And those who do not clothe the naked when they have the power to do so, should they not be called the same? The bread you are holding back is for the hungry, the clothes you keep put away are for the naked, the shoes that are rotting away with disuse are for those who have none, the silver you keep buried in the earth is for the needy.

Basil of Caesarea, "I Will Tear Down My Barns"

Deborah Batt, *Further Development*

historical development, but as an invasion. The verdict has already been handed down. The final word has already been spoken. In Christ, the judgment has come. Christians are those, then, who are no longer at liberty to imagine or desire any social or political or economic order other than the *koinonia* of the early church, no other communal morality than the anarchy of Christian love.

Of course, the political import of this truth – at least, as regards action in the present – must still be sought. As I said at the beginning, I have no answer ready to hand. But, as I also said, we can at least define our terms. And we can certainly identify which political and social realities must be abhorrent to a Christian conscience: a cultural ethos that not only permits but encourages a life of ceaseless acquisition as a kind of moral good; a legal regime subservient to the corporatist imperative of maximum profits, no matter what the methods employed or consequences produced; a politics of cruelty, division, national identity, or any of the countless ways in which we contrive to demarcate the sphere of what is rightfully "ours" and not "theirs."

Before all else, we must pursue a vision of the common good (by whatever charitable means we can) that presumes that the basis of law and justice is not the inviolable right to private property, but rather the more original truth taught by men such as Basil the Great, Gregory of Nyssa, Ambrose of Milan, and John Chrysostom: that the goods of creation belong equally to all, and that immense private wealth is theft – bread stolen from the hungry, clothing stolen from the naked, money stolen from the destitute.

But how to pursue a truly Christian politics at this hour – at least, assuming we hope actually to alter the shape of society – is an altogether more difficult question, and one that perhaps we shall be able to address only if we have truly first learned to disabuse ourselves of the material assumptions that capitalism has taught us to harbor over many generations.

Even so, in light of the judgment that entered human time in Christ, a Christian is allowed to long and hope ultimately for no other society than one that is truly communist and anarchist, in the very special way in which the early church was both at once. Even now, in the time of waiting, whoever does not truly imagine such a society and desire it to come into being has not the mind of Christ. ➤

The Interim God

Forget religion versus secularism.
The battle is mammon versus humanity.

EBERHARD ARNOLD

In October 1924, five years after the German Revolution, Plough's *founding editor, Eberhard Arnold, gave a speech in a small mining town in Saxony, Germany, to a working-class audience. This article is based on that talk.*

ACCORDING TO the ancient Persian prophet Zoroaster, two opposing powers are active in this world. These powers are not inseparably divided between "this world" versus "the other world," spirit versus matter. Rather, they are opposing poles challenging one another: good and evil, life and death, light and darkness, obscurity and clarity, the contrast between day and night.

There are many who believe that religious people, the idealists, the devout, are on one side in this struggle, while materialists, those concerned with outward things, are on the other side. Certainly, this classification appears justified. But it misses the point.

Amedeo Modigliani, *Study of a Head*

Eberhard Arnold (1883–1935) was a German theologian and cofounder of the Bruderhof.

The great struggle takes place in the heart of every person – in every materialist just as much as in every religious person. We cannot say that the good are on one side and the bad on the other, nor is it true that the religious life is good while the materialist life is bad. The important thing is to discern where materialist thinking puts its faith, and where religious life finds its god – where the spirit of each is found and what each values.

In religion as well as in atheism there is an antigod whom we can worship. The early Christians were convinced that there is a god in the world who is not the God of Jesus Christ. There is a god of godless, worldly religion, antagonistic to the life of Jesus; a god of the present era, hostile to God's future.

The nature of this antigod is work without soul, business without love, machinery without spirit, and lust instead of joy. It craves for possessions without mutual help, destroys competitors, and idolizes private property, obtained through fraud. It is a god of the present age, an interim god. This demonic force is at work even in the most religious places, where devotion wears its most pious mask.

We read in early Christian writings that a god of this world has blinded the minds of those who cannot believe and are perishing. It has corrupted their vision so that they are no longer able to see what really matters. Jesus, the leader of the coming age, declared war on this spirit. He spoke of this fight and of certain victory when he said, "You cannot serve two masters. You cannot serve God and mammon."

What Is Mammon?

We would not be able to understand the term *mammon* unless we knew the other names by which Jesus exposes this spirit. He calls it the "murderer from the beginning" and "the father of lies," and refers to its emissaries as "unclean spirits" (John 8:44; Matt. 10:1). Mammonism is its nature, murder its trade, lying its character, and impurity its face.

To the moralist, these four traits may seem unrelated, but in truth there is no fundamental difference. Mammonism is the covetous will: to seize, possess, and enjoy. Thus, these apparently different designations – mammon, lying, murder, and immorality – disclose one and the same spirit, one and the same god. The reality around us shows the enormous power this god possesses in the world.

Jesus says: Lay up no treasure for yourself on earth; sell all you have and give to the poor, and come, and go a totally new way with me (Matt. 6:19; Luke 18:22). Wealth works as a curse because it stands in the way of liberation. It is an affliction because it burdens and satiates but cannot fulfill. Private property kills friendship and gives rise to injustice. "Woe to you that are rich, woe to you that are full." "Blessed are you that are poor" (Luke 6:20, 24).

There has to be a great turning point, when true friendship will be won by giving away property, when fellowship will be found by turning away from injustice. "Make friends for yourselves through unjust mammon" (Luke 16:9). Win hearts by giving away all you own. Go the new way of fellowship and community given by the Spirit; seek the unity that comes from God and penetrates through the soul into material things. Flee from mammon and turn to God!

Commodities and Money

On hearing the word *mammon* we think of money first of all. And indeed money is the most tangible symbol of mammonism. Mammon means valuing wealth and converting human relationships into material values.

Life is relationship, interaction, giving and receiving, coming and going, and daily working side by side. People are called to fellowship of emotion and will, of knowledge and creative work, of faith and hope. They are called to a fellowship of life.

But here is money – the mightiest power in the present world system – that stifles and obstructs this fellowship. Everything that would otherwise be a living interchange, a service of mutual help, becomes a dead coin, a piece of paper. Money in itself is not evil, but the way it swallows up what is living in man's spirit is evil. This, then, is the satanic nature of money: we have financial relationships that are no longer personal, no longer part of a fellowship of faith and life. People buy and pay for each other. They consume the commodities they have purchased without any care about the people who produced them.

Money contains all the work and effort of people whom we neither know nor care about. It makes people forget the mutual exchange that takes place in work done and services rendered. The spirit of fellowship in our relationships is reified: it is conjured into a thing which is its opposite.

Today it's impossible for an employer in a gigantic factory to establish a relationship with the workers and to care about them personally, though in terms of money he has a clearly defined relationship to them. For the shareholders in a limited-liability corporation, this is even less likely. The mutual relationship between the investors and those who do the work has been eliminated by the shareholding structure, the board of directors, and the management, all pushed between investor and worker. No one is personally responsible for what happens to the worker. The shareholder can defer to the board of directors, and the board of directors can defer to the shareholders. Profits and balance sheets are the first priorities; the worker counts only as a wage statistic.

"Did not all the prophets speak from hearts as troubled as mine? Did not the same anger flare up in them against the horde that denied the earth – open to all – to others, by laws and verdicts, as by a sorcerous spell? Make the earth free again for us; it is the victim of madmen now."

—Zoroaster

Wherever and whenever this happens we have fallen prey to mammon – that is, to Satan.

Nicholas Roerich, *Book of Wisdom*

Is Communism the Answer?

This is why in our hyper-capitalistic era we urgently need the counter-symbol of a man like Francis of Assisi, who chose voluntary poverty and rejected money. People often react with indignation to those who, like the saint, refuse to touch money out of love and for the sake of freedom. Yet this very reaction shows how necessary such a symbolic step into economic impossibility actually is in order to destroy

Image from Wikimedia Commons (public domain)

"And even if our gospel is veiled, it is veiled to those who are perishing. The god of this age has blinded the minds of unbelievers, so that they cannot see the light of the gospel that displays the glory of Christ, who is the image of God. For what we preach is not ourselves, but Jesus Christ as Lord, and ourselves as your servants for Jesus' sake."

—2 Corinthians 4:3–5

Nicholas Roerich, *Shadows*

the illusion of money's all-dominating power within mammonism.

In the end, both money and the rejection of money are only symbols for the realities that stand behind them. The god mammon is not identical with money or private property (though the Spirit overcomes both), nor will rejecting money or sharing in common ownership necessarily bring people into God's kingdom of love (though God's will is for us to do both). Indeed, mammon is in communism as well as in capitalism. For old-school Marxists, the economic need of the dispossessed – their bread-and-butter requirements for food, clothing, and housing – is the only driving force in human history and society. Accordingly, they believe that in the struggle for existence, the war of the have-nots against the haves must be waged to the end. In this view, our whole life is a material one and arises automatically out of the instincts of self-preservation and reproduction.

This way of thinking is still mammonism. For if we build our mutual relationships only on the requirements of food, clothing, shelter, and sex, then we are basing our lives on a reification of the spirit no less than in capitalism.

All the same, there is a great and deep truth in the protest that arises from Marxism. What motivates this movement for social justice is not primarily dialectic materialism, or the economic interpretation of history, or the theory of surplus value, or the transition from capitalism to a socialist state enterprise via trusts. It is not even the goal of collective ownership. No, the driving force of this movement is faith in the ultimate future of justice, in the victory of a fellowship that will extend to material things, embracing everything. The hidden force behind Marxist materialism is a revolt of the spirit in the name of matter; it is a mass attack on the mammonism of those "spiritual" people who have the spirit on their lips but materialism in their desires.

Conversely, even among wealthy people the reifying of relationships through money can be overcome – often in a patriarchal way, but sometimes in a fraternal one – through the just administration of goods for the benefit of all. Faith in an ultimate future of justice can be alive among capitalists; it can be alive in materialists and socialists; for it can live in the heart that seeks love and believes in a just future. If we feel this, then we can be convinced – like Zoroaster – that there is a power of good, which is stronger, at all times and in all places, than the force of mammonism.

This World, This Life

We must get rid of the idea that the kingdom Jesus proclaimed is purely otherworldly, that his intention was to make good someday in heaven all that is bad on earth. If that were so, we would have to become otherworldly people who long above all for the hour of death – people like those monks who lie in their coffins every day to prepare for dying. Death would then be the liberator, giving us the final kiss to freedom from the shackles of this shameful existence and lifting us out of bodily life into a paradise of pure, ethereal joys.

We must reject any such notion energetically. The great division between God and the devil is not the division between life here and life beyond, between matter and spirit, between corporeality and incorporeality – no, it runs right through all spirits and all bodies, through all eternities and all times. In every body, every human being, both powers are at work. Both operate in every age and moment of history, including this one now.

The decisive question is: how will the spirit of life come to rule in each person, in each moment, in each body, and throughout the whole planet Earth? And how will mammon, the demon of covetousness and injustice, be conquered and eliminated?

Brothers and sisters, love the earth. Brothers and sisters, be true to the earth, and do not believe those seducers who look longingly to the world beyond, casting suspicion on this world. Jesus is the greatest friend of the earth – Jesus who again and again, in the original spirit of Judaism, proclaimed love for this earth, love for the soil, love for the land. Blessed are the peacemakers, for they shall possess the earth.

In Zoroaster's writing we find the combination of truth, purity, and work on the land as the basic promise for divine life. Jesus, like the Jewish prophets, proclaims that God's creative rulership will burst in upon this earth, inaugurating a new era. This earth shall become a garden of justice, truth, and purity of mutual relationships. Then the joy of life that God intends will begin on this planet.

Jesus says simply: What you want people to do for you, do for them (Matt. 7:12). Make sure that all others have what you think you need yourself. The distribution of land, work, and goods should be in harmony with the justice of God, who lets the sun shine and the rain fall on the just and the unjust (Matt. 5:45).

This is not a matter of a future utopia in some far-off place. On the contrary, the certainty of this future is a present power. God is alive today, and his spirit will one day unite all people. The same divine spark lives in every human being. The poet Schiller describes it in his "Ode to Joy" as the brotherly love that embraces all the world's millions.

However sharp their differences, this is the one thing that should unite all political factions, Christians and non-Christians: the inner certainty that everything must be completely different, that what destroys solidarity and shatters trust will in the end be overcome by joy in life and fellowship in justice. For the faith we hold is in a living God. ➴

This article is condensed from the text of the original speech; a longer version appears in Eberhard Arnold, Salt and Light *(Plough, 1998).*

I Begin with a Little Girl's Hair

G. K. CHESTERTON

Bianca Berends, *Postcard Redhead Girl in Green*

I BEGIN WITH a little girl's hair. That I know is a good thing at any rate. Whatever else is evil, the pride of a good mother in the beauty of her daughter is good. It is one of those adamantine tendernesses which are the touch-stones of every age and race. If other things are against it, other things must go down. If landlords and laws and sciences are against it, landlords and laws and sciences must go down. With the red hair of one she-urchin in the gutter I will set fire to all modern civilization. Because a girl should have long hair, she should have clean hair; because she should have clean hair, she should not have an unclean home: because she should not have an unclean home, she should have a free and leisured mother; because she should have a free mother, she should not have an usurious landlord; because there should not be an usurious landlord, there should be a redistribution of property; because there should be a redistribution of property, there shall be a revolution. That little urchin with the gold-red hair, whom I have just watched toddling past my house, she shall not be lopped and lamed and altered; her hair shall not be cut short like a convict's; no, all the kingdoms of the earth shall be hacked about and mutilated to suit her. She is the human and sacred image; all around her the social fabric shall sway and split and fall; the pillars of society shall be shaken, and the roofs of ages come rushing down, and not one hair of her head shall be harmed. ⌁

Source: *What's Wrong with the World* (London: Cassel, 1910).

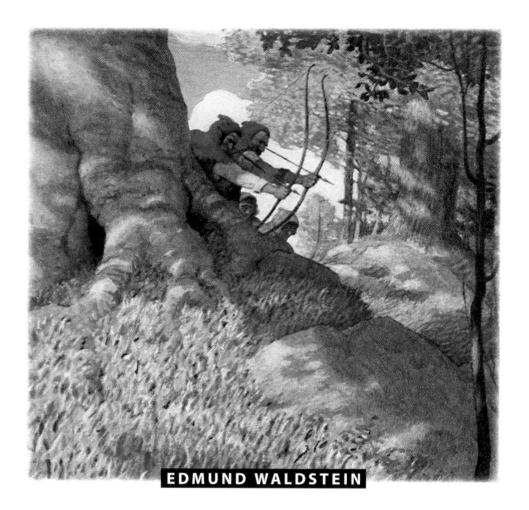

EDMUND WALDSTEIN

Robin Hood Economics

The goods of the earth
belong to everyone.

ONCE, WHEN THE SHERIFF of Nottingham's men came across Robin Hood deep in Sherwood Forest, he was kneeling before an altar, hearing Mass. Robin waited until the holy sacrifice was over before turning to fight them. The old ballads consistently describe Robin as a pious and faithful Catholic, scrupulously chaste, who was said to have heard three Masses every day before breakfast. In fact, Robin's band of merry men is described as following a quasi-monastic rule. They shared a common purse. And according to the sixteenth-century play *The Downfall of Robert, Earle of Huntingdon*, based on older ballads, they even took a vow of chastity: "Thirdly no yeoman following Robin Hoode / In Sherewood, shall use widowe, wife, or maid, / But by true labour, lustfull thoughts expell."

Previous page and next:
N. C. Wyeth, details of illustrations for Paul Creswick's *Robin Hood*

Nevertheless Robin loved to rob the abbots and priors of England's rich, feudal monasteries: "From wealthy abbots' chests, and churls' abundant store, / What oftentimes he took, he shar'd amongst the poor." Those monasteries practiced a certain kind of poverty – they held everything in common, and each monk was to receive only what was necessary from the common stock – yet, corporately, they were rich landowners, and their abbots and priors were influential lords.

The monasteries gave much to the poor, providing a kind of social security. (Indeed, the dissolution of the monasteries by Henry VIII was to lead to a social crisis.) Yet to Robin Hood they were on the side of the rich who take an unfair share of the crops produced by peasants. The only religious whom Robin seemed to like were the mendicant friars, such as Friar Tuck, who were the proponents of a new interpretation of religious poverty, in which there was to be no corporate wealth.

The world described in the Robin Hood ballads of the fifteenth century, when the feudal system was in its post–Black Death decline, is obviously very different from our own world of global capitalism. And yet, Robin Hood can in some ways be a spur to reflection on our own situation.

The implicit foundation of Robin Hood's stealing from the rich to give to the poor is the perennial Christian teaching that the goods of the earth are given by God for the sustenance of all human beings. This is the principle that modern Catholic social teaching calls the "universal destination of goods," and it issues an urgent challenge to us in our own time.

As a Cistercian monk, I find that Robin's contempt for the monasteries of his time raises questions for me about the relation of my monastic community, with its communal sharing of goods, to the wider economic order. This is a question that any community of believers that tries to live like the early Church in Acts 2:44–45 will have to ask: How can we interact with the wider economic system that surrounds us without becoming complicit in the injustices of that system?

JESUS' INJUNCTIONS on giving freely and without expectation of return fulfill and complete the teachings of the Old Testament. God gave the earth to all humankind. To give to those in need, therefore, is an act of justice, rendering to them what they are due as those to whom God has given the earth.

After the conversion of Constantine, as more of society became Christian and being Christian became less a countercultural choice, the Fathers of the Church were very concerned with correcting wealthy Christians who had

---

Edmund Waldstein, O.Cist., is a monk of Stift Heiligenkreuz, a Cistercian abbey in Austria.

lost sight of this principle and were withholding their wealth from those in need. Saint Basil the Great in the East and Saint Ambrose of Milan in the West were particularly insistent on the point. Thus, Basil addresses the rich man in Luke 12:18, who says "This is what I shall do: I shall tear down my barns and build larger ones. There I shall store all my grain and other goods and I shall say to myself, 'Now as for you, you have so many good things stored up for many years, rest, eat, drink, be merry!'" To this man Saint Basil retorts, "Tell me, what things are yours? Where did you take them from? Did you give them being?" The grain that has grown does not really belong to the rich man; it is for those who need it. Similarly, Saint Ambrose preached a sermon on the story of King Ahab's coveting of Naboth's vineyard in which he addressed himself directly to the rich citizens of Milan with searching questions: "How far, O rich, do you extend your mad greed? . . . Why do you cast out the companion whom nature has given you and claim for yourself nature's possession? The earth was established in common for all, rich and poor. Why do you alone, O rich, demand special treatment?" It is unjust, Ambrose thinks, for the rich to claim the fruits of the earth for themselves exclusively, when that bounty was given to humankind in common.

> **I must admit that Robin Hood would probably disapprove of me.**

In the light of these teachings of scripture and the Church Fathers, the scholastic theologians questioned whether the possession of private property in any sense can be justified.

Saint Thomas Aquinas argued that while the *use* or *enjoyment* of goods always has to be common, in the sense that each person only gets to use or consume what they need, the system of *producing* goods can be private, in the sense that each person can dispose of what they produce. In fact, he gives reasons why it is conducive to a peaceful and just society for there to be private property in that qualified sense. He thinks that people tend to work harder when they have responsibility for what they produce. He gives the example of a household in which there are too many servants: in this case, some of them will not bother to work for the common store, since they can depend on the others to work for them: "Every man is more careful to procure what is for himself alone than that which is common to many or to all: since each one would shirk the labor and leave to another that which concerns the community, as happens where there is a great number of servants." The experience of the socialist regimes of the twentieth century confirms Saint Thomas's insight here.

He also argues that things are more orderly when there is private property, whereas

as the rule commanded, because they had serfs to work for them. Not surprisingly, the serfs sometimes resented their monastic overlords, and thought that they took an unjust share of the produce of the serfs' labor.

My own order, the Cistercian order, was founded partly in reaction to that problem. The Cistercians wanted to return to a literal observance of the rule, living from their own manual labor. Nevertheless, even in the Cistercian order, the greater part of the manual labor was soon done by the illiterate "lay brothers" (peasants who had entered the monastery) while the educated "choir brothers" (recruited from the gentry) were more engaged in intellectual labor – copying manuscripts, teaching, writing theological treatises – and in more frequent formal prayer. Moreover, when they were given lands to found a monastery, the people giving the lands would often relocate the serfs who had been there before. My monastery was founded in 1133 when Saint Leopold III, margrave of Austria, donated some of his feudal possessions for our foundation. In the woods behind our monastery one can still see a few stone walls belonging to a village whose inhabitants were relocated when our monastery was founded. I often wonder what the serfs who lived there thought when they had to leave their home. Later on, the Cistercians, too, ruled over peasant inhabitants in their territories.

TODAY, my monastery still has many of the lands that were given to us in the Middle Ages, and we live principally from the timber, grain, and wine grown on them. A few monks still work the land, but on account of various necessities through the centuries, most of the monks now "work" as parish priests in nearby parishes, or as teachers in our theological college (as I do). But this means that most of the work in our forests, fields, and vineyards is now done by wage labor. Our workers and employees like to quote the old saying, "life is good under a crooked staff" – meaning that clerical masters (symbolized by the pastoral staff or crozier) are more lenient than lay ones. In fact, we try to follow Catholic social teaching in treating those we employ; we pay them a living wage, and so on.

But this sometimes leads to difficult situations. For example, we used to have a sawmill to process the timber from our forests. If we could have worked the sawmill entirely with the labor of monks, it would have been profitable, but since we had to employ wage laborers, and since we paid them a living wage, it could not compete with the large-scale sawmills run by competitor corporations. Eventually, after losing money on the sawmill for several years, we decided to close it down. It was a difficult decision, and the difficulty arose from the almost inevitable necessity of interacting with the larger capitalist system that surrounds us. The system has its own dynamic, which is hard to escape.

ACCORDING TO the principle of the universal destination of goods, *all* superfluous goods belong by right to the poor. But the difficulty comes in determining what really is superfluous. The human heart is devious, and skilled in self-deception. It is perhaps easier for communities to judge objectively about this than individuals. But even in communities one can find what Eberhard Arnold, cofounder of the Bruderhof, called "collective egoism."

My own experience of living out community of goods in the monastery has been a liberating one. Since I receive everything that I need from the monastery I am free to devote myself to prayer, to teaching theology, and to my other duties. But I must admit that Robin Hood would probably disapprove of me. Although

my monastery tries to give away as much of our income as possible, nevertheless we monks live fairly comfortable lives, with good food and warm rooms. Saint Benedict lists the necessary things that a monk should receive from the abbot: two cowls, two tunics, sandals, shoes, a girdle, a knife, a pen, a needle, a handkerchief, and a writing tablet. I'm afraid that in addition to cowl and tunic I have coats, jackets, socks, skiing equipment, and so on. That writing tablet has now become a laptop. I am even given a monthly allowance of pocket money for buying books, chocolate, and other luxuries.

But, of course, whether Robin Hood would approve of us or not, we are grateful for the good things that God gives. The primary purpose of monastic poverty is not to despise the gifts that God has given to humankind, but to conform ourselves to Christ. There is a time for fasting and doing penance, but there is also a time for feasting, and using the goods of the earth to express joy. "For John came neither eating nor drinking, and they say, 'He

has a demon'; the Son of Man came eating and drinking, and they say, 'Behold, a glutton and a drunkard'" (Matt. 11:18–19).

This was a lesson that the early Cistercians had to learn. In the early years of Saint Bernard's monastery at Clairvaux, the monks were unwilling to eat anything that tasted good. But when William of Champeaux, the Bishop of Châlons-sur-Marne, visited them, he taught them to accept their food with thanksgiving: "You will be safe in doing so, for through God's grace it has become fit for you to use. On the other hand, if you still remain disobedient and incredulous, you will be resisting the Holy Spirit and so be ungrateful for his grace."

In the old ballads, Robin Hood is famous for his generous woodland feasts. So on this point at least, he and the bishop would have seen eye to eye. ➤

N. C. Wyeth, detail of an illustration for Paul Creswick's *Robin Hood*

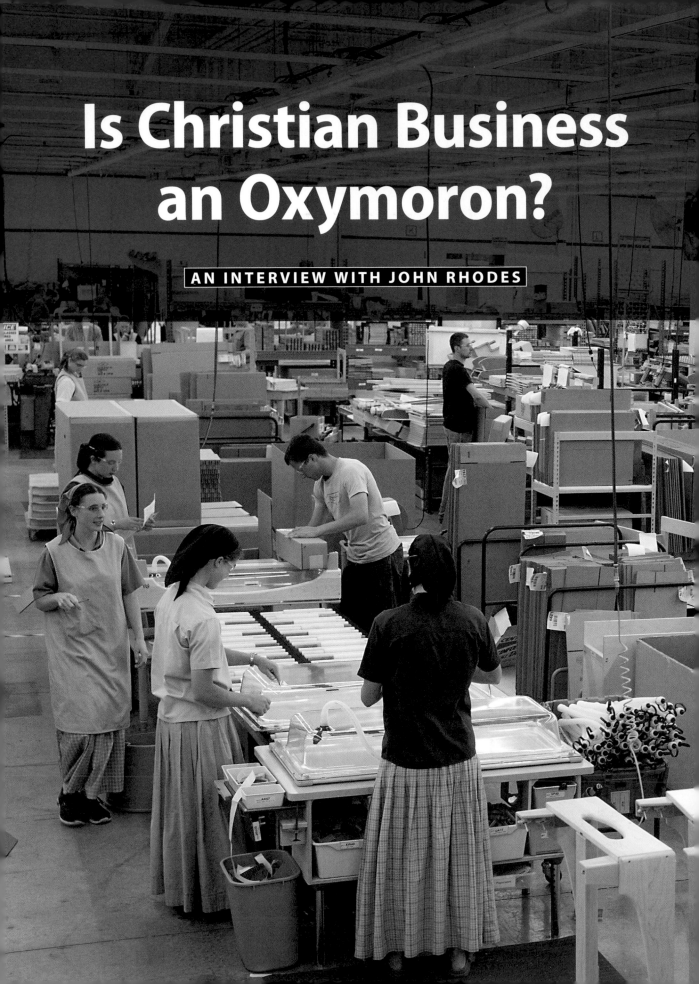

Is Christian Business an Oxymoron?

AN INTERVIEW WITH JOHN RHODES

"From each according to his ability, to each according to his need."

Marx's slogan sounds hopelessly utopian as a business strategy. But is it? For decades the Bruderhof communities have operated businesses with this motto – successfully. *Plough* **interviewed John Rhodes, who led these businesses for twenty years, about the nuts and bolts of running a communal company.**

Plough: Tell us a little about the Bruderhof's businesses.

John Rhodes: Community Playthings has been manufacturing wooden toys and school furniture since 1947. Forty years ago, it launched a line of therapeutic equipment for children with disabilities, now called Rifton Equipment. These two businesses provide a livelihood for most of the three thousand adults and children who live in the twenty-five Bruderhof communities worldwide. They support Bruderhof schools, outreach, and publishing, including *Plough*. And they make possible the Bruderhof's humanitarian work, helping locally, responding to disasters, and contributing money or manpower to organizations such as Samaritan's Purse and Save the Children.

But what's really unusual about these businesses is that while they sell into the marketplace, internally they're run communally. There are no bosses or employees, and everyone gets the same pay: nothing. We see our work as our contribution to a life in which we share everything as the first Christians did.

John Rhodes is director of development for Community Playthings and Rifton Equipment.

Does that make for a truly Christian way of doing business?

No, it doesn't. At least, that's the answer my mentor and predecessor Tom Potts always gave. Tom came from a Philadelphia Quaker family and had run a steel business before joining the Bruderhof. People would ask him: "How do you run a Christian business?" Tom always answered, "We don't. A Christian business is an oxymoron. When the kingdom of heaven comes to earth, there will be no money-making and no businesses."

To an extent, we operate like every other company. We pick a market and find an unfulfilled need. We design a product to meet that need and market it in a way that costs us less than people are willing to pay.

The difference is the context behind the business: a life of brotherhood. These are brothers and sisters working together out of a common conviction – and having a lot of fun doing it!

Is this socialism?

Some might call it that, but I don't believe in state control of the economy. The right question is, "What would the economics of love

A production workshop for Community Playthings, a Bruderhof company

Photographs by James Clarke. Used with permission.

look like?" We try to live in such a way that our life answers that question.

Meaningful Work for Everyone

So what's it like to be a worker in this kind of business?

Most businesses seek to maximize income and minimize the number of employees. Our task is to find the right variety of work so that everyone can meaningfully contribute, as we make enough income to build up the community. In our workshops, there's work for everyone, old or young, male or female, guest or long-time member, skilled or unskilled, disabled or able-bodied, whether you come expected or unannounced. You're welcomed and there's a place for you to work.

While there's no such thing as a Christian business, there is Christian work – or rather, work is a good part of being human. It would

be presumptuous to say what the kingdom of God will be like, but I do believe that there will still be work. We will work to serve others. So work in the Bruderhof models the work of the future kingdom. Our work is an expression of the brotherly and sisterly community to which we're called. Admittedly, putting a nut onto a bolt may not feel very meaningful. But if it's done in the spirit of love, it takes on meaning.

In our workshops, you will see older folk doing physically easier work in a quieter area. We intentionally hang on to work that could be outsourced or automated, because when an eighty-year-old comes to the shop, she wants to put in a meaningful day's work that actually supports the community's mission.

The phrase "the tragedy of the commons," referring to abuse or neglect of shared resources, is used to dismiss communal ways of living and working together. Is that a problem?

It's a real problem. If everybody owns something, then nobody owns it, and things are not always cared for. But individual ownership has also produced bad fruits: as soon as you own something, you have to protect it, then you have inequality, envy, theft, and war.

One of the legitimate criticisms leveled at socialism is that when you remove private ownership, people are not motivated to work. Why should I put my best effort in if everyone gets paid the same in the end anyway? But in reality, money is a surprisingly poor motivator. A much stronger motivator is purpose. Motivation in our context doesn't come from state mandates or financial self-interest – it comes from our calling to live in community.

Another motivator for people is status, right?

That might generally be true. But we're not defined by the type of work we do. If your work has unequal pay, then it's easier to think of some people as "more valuable." But for us the person programming a computer is not of higher value than someone putting on a knob or driving in a screw.

Then there's the question of bosses. Even in a fast-food restaurant, if you have a management position, you may not earn much more than the people flipping burgers, but you can at least boss them around. That's something not really present with us.

Jesus says that the people of this world lord it over each other, but it should not be that way among us. If you walk into our workshop you will not very easily be able to tell who's in charge. Yes, the work has to get done, but we're in that together. If the person who was asked to be responsible for the shop were authoritarian or uncaring, we would find him another job. And that's how we do our work everywhere in the community; things aren't different just because this is the income-earning portion of our work.

The Community Comes First

Do the imperatives of the business ever clash with the needs of the community?

Many times we've taken a direction with our business that was not a good business decision but was a good community decision. For example, in the early days of Community Playthings we distributed via hundreds of school supply dealers, offering them discounts. It was like adding five hundred sales people to our team.

A decade or so after the business started, it was overheating. We were six months behind fulfilling orders. The business was pushing the community. And there was pushback: after talking it through in a meeting, the community decided that Tom, my predecessor, needed to slow the business down. This was difficult;

growth is business's natural evolution. And at that time we badly needed the money that these orders were bringing in.

Any normal business would hire more people, build more factories, and ride the crest of that wave. But we don't hire workers. From a business standpoint, the worst thing we could do would be to drop the dealers' discounts. Tom told me it was the most difficult business decision he ever had to make. But he did it at the request of the community. The business took a big hit, but it also recovered, and grew in a way that served the community's needs rather than sucking the life from it.

This is one way we fight against mammon, the power of money. We seek efficiency in our shops, but there is a limit. When we bump up against this limit, we decrease the demand on those who are working. We skip a catalog mailing, drop products, or raise prices.

The Bruderhof community places a high value on spontaneity and being led by the Spirit. Does that ever conflict with good business planning?

We've repeatedly run into the issue of too much organization. A business needs order, but if we are inwardly dead then this order becomes pure bureaucratic organization and takes on a life of its own, squashing the sense of fraternity in our work and ruling our life.

Most people who are responsible for a business have control over two important things: human resources and financial resources. I had control over neither of those things. If the community decides that my operations manager is needed for mission work abroad, he goes and I have to figure it out. And I can't go out and hire anybody else. By the same token, I can't fire anyone either. If there's a problem, a change of assignment may be necessary, but

we're still committed to living and working together. So if there's anything between us personally, we have to work it out.

Or I may go to the community and say we'd like to purchase a piece of equipment. The community may say, well, there's been a cyclone in Bangladesh and we just gave away a chunk of money, so not this year. And we say OK.

Often, if we have a big order to fill, members who normally do other work – on the farm, in the medical clinic, or for *Plough* – will come help out in the factory. Other times, say if there's a harvest to get in or a neighborhood event to support, everyone working in the shop will leave to do that. And sometimes the whole community knocks off to have a picnic or play softball. At times like that, it can look like it's going to be tough to get the work done. But this keeps the business from becoming a money-making machine that gobbles up all the community's energy.

How does work–life balance play out in the community context?

There are strong community norms about keeping work in its place. We go home at five o'clock. Parents will drop their work if there's a school event. And nobody brings a laptop home to catch up on email while the kids are home.

Too often people compartmentalize. Their work life is here and their family there, their religious life one way and their social life another. But everything we do is one fabric. I'm living the brotherly life whether I'm in the shop, at home, or in the school. The work in the business is not so important that I have to drag it into everything else I do.

We say whatever is good for the community will be good for the business. And this is important because money has a power of its own. You can't serve God and money. So we're serving God and utilizing money; the money must always be subservient to the cause for which we live.

Interacting with Capitalism

Is there any conflict between this internal culture and the need to survive in the marketplace?

Of course; we're living in a capitalistic environment. Still, we try to bring the best of our approach to life into that environment, rather than letting it shape us. So, for example, in our sales work we don't put people on the road much. We want to be together, and we don't want fathers and mothers to be away from their children as a regular part of their job. So that means basically we work with phones and digital communication.

It's not in most Bruderhof members' social skill set to convince people to part with their money. But they are comfortable relating with people. The markets we're in, education and health care, are largely about children. We love children, and have lots of them in our communities. Our toys were designed by fathers and mothers making things for their own kids.

When our folks talk to people on the phone, they talk to them as human beings, not as potential customers. We may run into a mom who has had to fight all her life for her child with disabilities, so she may start out instinctively combative. We listen. Pretty soon she realizes that we're actually on her side. These are universal principles of how people should treat each other. Other people aren't always motivated by money either. We connect with people in a way that affirms their dignity and humanity, and then the money takes care of itself.

In our capitalist economy, technology allows fewer workers to be more productive. How do you deal with that dynamic?

We look at its inner effect. We have to balance efficiency with meeting the work requirements of the community. A guest can walk into our shop and be productive after a few minutes of training and doesn't need to be intimidated by some complex machine. We're slow to automate a process.

Technology often tends to work against community. For example, once we had to dig a ditch about a hundred feet long between two buildings. One person could have easily dug that ditch with a backhoe in an hour. Instead we got twenty-five brothers with shovels and picks. It probably took us twice as long, but it was a great communal experience and we enjoyed being together. Wendell Berry talks about demanding circumstances, how technology often removes the demand and makes our lives more convenient, which works against our character and makes us flabby. Obviously, we have to find the right balance; it's not that we don't use technology, but we try to use it judiciously.

In recent years the world's biggest companies have also discovered the business value of "community" and "teamwork" in getting the most out of their employees. Is there any difference between what you're describing and the management practices of a Silicon Valley firm?

Teamwork used as a business principle is an artificial thing. We work together because we love one another and enjoy being together. It's more than teamwork: it's a relationship with brothers and sisters. And because of this, working through conflicts is vital. If two people are having a disagreement, the work will stop until it is resolved because the relationship is more important.

What really breaks down relationships is backbiting. Being upfront is the best way to form deeper friendships. And in all these things, living rightly ends up being better for

the business too: tensions reduce productivity; you end up with hard feelings and turf wars, and everything goes down the drain.

A friend who's a business owner once told me that the Bruderhof combines the best aspects of socialism – equality, brotherhood, meaningful work for all – with the best aspects of capitalism, especially entrepreneurship, creativity, and strong work ethic.

People are creative by nature. When they are freed from workplace tensions and from worry about money, they are free to be who they are. For example, even in your area of a production workshop, you can be creative in terms of making improvements or changes.

If all the work is meaningful, then blossoming doesn't mean climbing the corporate ladder. Instead, we're ambitious to serve. How can I make more of a contribution? There are hundreds of different tasks, and work and hobbies outside the businesses as well. There's always opportunity to learn more, not selfishly but so one can better contribute and serve. That fosters creativity and an entrepreneurial spirit.

What Is Money Good For?

The Bruderhof's businesses are successful. What challenges does that pose?

One of the challenges of running a community business is that it may do too well. Many monastic orders have struggled with this. Success can pose a challenge to our inner life. We may become wasteful, selfish, or start accumulating things for ourselves. We may get proud because we think this is all our own accomplishment. We may depend less on God. It's very important that we thank God every day for providing us with this daily bread. Gratitude helps us avoid some of the inner dangers of too much income.

A major question is what to do with the income. The money doesn't belong to us: it belongs to God and we have to use it for his purposes. If we use it to feather our own nest, that is a sin. We've chosen voluntary poverty and don't want to accumulate goods for ourselves. So we don't actually keep a lot of cash on hand unless we're building up a reserve for a major project, like the purchase of property for a new community. In general, when we have extra funds, we give them away.

Yes, earning money in the market economy is to some extent a compromise. If this starts affecting our community's life, we have to recognize these things early enough and take steps against them. Because of our fallen nature, there will always be some tendency toward selfishness. But we recognize that as the enemy and so we're constantly on guard to help one another stay true to that vision.

A few years ago in the woodshop, an older brother named Josef Stängl approached me with a piece of wood he'd pulled from the trash. He handed it to me and said, "Eberhard [Arnold, the Bruderhof's cofounder] would never have allowed this to be thrown away." The wood had a defect; someone had decided it would take too much work to repair. From an economic viewpoint, the wood belonged in the bin. The time it would take to make the wood useable would have "cost" more than replacing it with a better piece of wood. But Josef was also right. He had an attitude of stewardship for the things of the earth. What attitude were we passing on to the next generation by throwing away this wood? Not that every piece of wood can be salvaged, but so much of what is produced in the world today is disposable, even by design. We reject that idea of planned obsolescence. Our products typically last for decades, even with heavy use in a daycare setting.

What role does faith play in your business planning?

It's remarkable that these businesses have lasted for almost seventy years. We see that as a gift from God, not the result of our own planning and accomplishments. It often seemed like we just fumbled through and made decisions that turned out well, though we really didn't know if they would. But if we always take the attitude that what's best for the community and for people's souls will ultimately be best for the business, God will take care of us. We trust in that and pray every day for our daily bread. We feel that the life that has been laid before us comes straight out of the New Testament, the words and life of Jesus. We have trust that if we keep to that course and help one another, we don't need to worry about the future. ➤

Interview by Peter Mommsen on May 1, 2019.

Working Girls

Sweatshops never went away.

— MARIA HENGEVELD —

Laborers work at a garment factory in Bac Giang province, Vietnam, 2015.

WOMEN'S EMPOWERMENT SELLS. You-go-girl messages have been used to push everything from shoes to body wash to cars, and it certainly sells in the sports world. In February, Nike released its "Dream Crazier" commercial, featuring female athletes like Simone Biles, Serena Williams, and Megan Rapinoe, and an inspirational voiceover: ". . . a woman running a marathon was crazy. . . . A woman boxing was crazy. A woman dunking? Crazy. Coaching an NBA team. Crazy. A woman competing in a hijab, changing her sport, landing a double cork 1080, or winning twenty-three grand slams, having

a baby, and then coming back for more? Crazy, crazy, crazy, crazy, and crazy."

Nike's been at it for a while now. In fact, my interest in the brand was originally sparked several years ago when I learned about the "girl empowerment" programs that the Nike Foundation, the company's philanthropic arm (now the Nike Community Impact Fund), was promoting in emerging economies like Uganda and Ethiopia. These girl-power programs had made Nike quite popular among women's groups and development organizations. Was this the same Nike that in the mid-1990s had been attacked by feminists and labor activists

Maria Hengeveld is a writer and a PhD student at Cambridge University.

for the widespread abuse in its overseas factories? What about the women making Nike sneakers and T-shirts today? How empowered did they feel? In 2016 those questions took me to Vietnam, where I learned that, contrary to Nike's girl-power image, in reality its factories were still contradicting the freedom and empowerment its commercials celebrate.

I interviewed Hao and three of her colleagues on a hot afternoon in January 2016. I met the workers with an interpreter outside the single room Hao shares with her husband and children, in an industrial area close to Ho Chi Minh, Vietnam's largest city. We sat in a circle on the floor outside and talked about the women's work at a shoe factory that supplies sneakers to Nike.

Hao's story was typical of the eighteen workers, employed at five different Nike suppliers, whom I interviewed that month. She was exhausted by long days, immense work pressure, daily humiliations when her work was deemed too slow or faulty, and the stress of trying to make ends meet on low wages. By the end of the month, Hao often had to borrow money to pay her bills. "I sell lottery tickets during my lunch break," she said, to help pay off debts. This was a risky undertaking, however: "If my boss catches me selling them, he might fire me." Hao had sent her five-year-old daughter to her family in northern Vietnam because she couldn't afford to care for her.

The factory floor is the opposite of empowering. The women showed me wage stubs and factory rule books that revealed illegal wage penalties, excessive hours, and wages four times lower than what they needed to give their families a decent quality of life. Overtime was routine, they said, not voluntary. They weren't allowed to leave after their shifts when deadlines were tight, even though they had children to pick up from school. Of the ten mothers

with young children that I spoke with, six had sent at least one child away out of financial desperation and saw the child only once or twice a year. These women are caught in a Catch-22 of having their families torn apart in an effort to keep them together.

When I confronted Nike with my findings and asked them to respond to the women's grievances, they didn't seem surprised or particularly concerned. "Transformation takes time," they wrote me, suggesting that, while the jobs were not dignified or well-paid – or up to the standards of their "empowerment" campaigns – the labor standards in Vietnam's garment sector would eventually evolve to those in the developed world.

Nike is only one of many multinational brands and retailers, including Gap and H&M, that take part in a system *designed* to push down labor standards. Nike selected Vietnam, a country whose laws forbid independent labor rights groups and strikes, as its primary sourcing destination. The grievances and powerlessness of Hao and her colleagues are not an aberration but a calculated outcome of a system designed to repress workers' struggle for dignified jobs. By prioritizing low production costs and doing business with countries with the weakest labor protections, brands like Nike, Zara, Gap, and H&M create the high-pressure, disempowering environment described by Hao and her colleagues.

AS THE HISTORY of America's own garment industry shows, improvements in labor conditions have never "eventually evolved." Unions and strikes are vital. One of the most famous and effective strikes, the "Uprising of the Twenty Thousand," was led by Ukrainian immigrant Clara Lemlich in New York City in November 1909. Work had become unbearable for tens of thousands of workers, many of them teenage girls, toiling in sweatshops on the Lower East Side. Wages were as low as four dollars per week, work weeks exceeded sixty-five hours, factories were dangerous and unsanitary, and sexual harassment was rampant. Union organizers like Lemlich knew that the only way to demand a fair share of the profits and force their bosses to improve factory conditions was to use their collective power as workers to shut the industry down.

> **They weren't allowed to leave after their shifts when deadlines were tight, even though they had children to pick up from school.**

And that's what they did: for nearly three months, between twenty and thirty thousand garment workers braved the freezing New York winter and walked the streets of Lower Manhattan to demand what they deserved. As the feminist labor historian Annelise Orleck describes in her study, *Common Sense and a Little Fire*, the bosses, backed by the city's police, took all kinds of cruel and violent measures against the strikers. Seven hundred women were arrested during the strike, and city officials portrayed them as unruly, immoral, and ungrateful. Lemlich herself was arrested seventeen times and six of her ribs were broken by police clubs.

But, backed by their union, wealthy allies, and sympathetic media coverage, the women persisted. Contrary to what male union leaders thought possible at its outset, the strike achieved many of its goals, including union recognition, a fifty-two-hour workweek, and wage increases. The strike's success proved that collective action in the garment industry was both possible and effective, and set a wave of garment strikes in motion in other cities.

The Uprising's success played an important role in improving factory conditions in the industry. But its tragic failure played an important role as well. Several factory owners, including Max Blanck and Isaac Harris of the Triangle Shirtwaist Factory, refused the strikers' demands to fix safety hazards. On March 25, 1911, a year after the conclusion of the Uprising, a fire erupted on the eighth floor of the building, and one hundred forty-six Triangle workers, many of whom had participated in the Uprising, burned or jumped to their deaths.

The deaths of the Triangle fire and the wave of strikes triggered by the Uprising galvanized the labor movement and forced nationwide improvements in working conditions. As Annelise Orleck writes, Lemlich and her organizing colleagues "were at the center of a storm that by 1919 had brought half of all women garment workers into trade unions." Later, much of the progressive labor legislation President Franklin D. Roosevelt adopted was created or inspired by female labor rights advocates who had witnessed, or lost friends to, the fire. Improved conditions were not produced by inevitable evolution, but by the blood and courage of New York's garment workers.

TODAY, JUST AS IT DID a century ago, the garment production industry favors girls and women for employment. As the stereotype goes, women's "nimble fingers" are naturally equipped for fine assembly line work. More importantly, they are considered more docile and less likely to stir up trouble than men. As a factory personnel manager in Taiwan told the anthropologist Linda Gail Arrigo, "young male workers are too restless and impatient to do monotonous work with no career value. If displeased, they sabotage the machines and even threaten the foreman. But girls? At most, they cry a little."

How does this sexist understanding square with the militancy of Clara Lemlich and the tens of thousands who fought for their rights in the early twentieth century? It doesn't: garment workers have always fought for their rights. The difference between 1909 and today is that, whereas then violence against workers happened in front of New York City's shirtwaist-wearing middle and upper classes, today most collective actions by workers, and the methods used to crack down on them, happen largely out of consumers' sight.

The global subcontracting model creates essential distance between western brand managers placing orders and factory managers keeping labor costs as low as possible. The dirty work of union busting has been outsourced along with T-shirt side seams, and it has never been easier for brands to look the other way.

Despite these obstacles, garment workers in Vietnam, Bangladesh, and elsewhere have taken to the streets to demand dignified work and fair wages. In Vietnam in 2008, around twenty thousand workers from subcontracting factories that supplied Nike went on strike for better wages and working conditions. Management fired at least seven women for instigating collective action. When an underground labor group urged Nike to help the women get re-hired by putting pressure on their subcontractors, Charles Brown, Nike's then senior director of global corporate responsibility compliance, hid behind Vietnam's restrictive regime. "It is important," he wrote back, "for workers to understand the boundaries of their legal rights and the rights and obligations of the employer in Vietnam," including, he pointed out, the right of employers to fire striking workers when they don't report to work for five days. Brown makes the country's lack of labor rights sound like a regrettable

surprise. In reality, Nike had chosen Vietnam precisely because of workers' lack of tools to empower themselves.

THE HISTORY of Nike's supply chain and the outsourcing choices illustrate how the "race to the bottom" works under corporate globalization. One of Nike's first outsourcing destinations in the 1970s was South Korea, a country then under military rule, which allowed workers few opportunities to organize. As described at the time by Barbara Ehrenreich and Annette Fuentes in *Ms. Magazine* and by Ruth Pearson and Diane Elson in the *Feminist Review*, women workers, many living in overcrowded rooms near the factories, faced extremely grim conditions. A sewing-machine operator, Min Chong Suk, wrote of sixteen-hour workdays, starvation wages, and health hazards: "When [the apprentices] shake the waste threads from the clothes, the whole room fills with dust, and it is hard to breathe. Since we've been working in such dusty air, there have been increasing numbers of people getting tuberculosis, bronchitis, and eye disease." To Min Chong Suk, it seemed that "no one knows our blood dissolves into the threads and seams, with sighs and sorrow."

Attempts at collective action by Korean workers were violently squashed in at least one instance by "action squads" that, "armed with steel bars and buckets of human excrement," broke into the women's organizing office and "smashed the office equipment, and smeared the excrement over the women's bodies and in their hair, eyes, and mouths."

When the women succeeded, winning modest wage increases and even helping to bring down the military government, Nike let them down. "In response to South Korean women workers' newfound activist confidence," Cynthia Enloe writes, "the sneaker company and its subcontractors began shutting down a number of their South Korean factories in the late 1980s and 1990s. . . . Having lost that special kind of workplace control that only an authoritarian government could offer," Nike and other European and American sneaker executives moved on to Indonesia, China, and Thailand.

Most collective actions by workers, and the methods used to crack down on them, happen largely out of consumers' sight.

By the early 1990s, "sweat-shop exposés" of export factories in Indonesia, Vietnam, Thailand, Honduras, and other countries finally forced brands to confront the flip side of their outsourcing model: the risk of reputational damage. Consumers, it turned out, didn't want to wear shoes or shirts made in sweatshops, and found the hands-off approach of the outsourcing model unconscionable. Activist groups, students, and consumers held the brands responsible.

Nike initially denied responsibility. Why, they asked, should they be held responsible for the workplace practices of its Indonesian business partners? Nike, they argued, is a shoe company, not the United Nations. Besides, a spokesperson pointed out, "The wages may be small, but it's better than having no job." The alternative for these women, he suggested, would be "harvesting coconut meat in the tropical sun." While consumer pressure has motivated brands such as Nike to implement factory oversight systems (which have been criticized as weak, ineffective, and secretive by unions and labor rights experts) the argument that "a bad job is better than no job" is still frequently invoked to justify the conditions under which products and profits are made.

Nike is certainly not alone in this approach. In 2013, a *Huffington Post* reporter asked Biagio Chiarolanza, the CEO of the Italian fashion brand Benetton, about his company's role in the Rana Plaza factory collapse in Bangladesh – an industrial accident that cost over 1134 garment workers their lives and that, like the Triangle factory fire in 1911, would have been entirely preventable. Chiarolanza told the journalist that Benetton's subcontractors, not the company itself, were at fault. When viewed in isolation from the supply chain as a whole, this argument might be convincing to some. But when the suffering and exploitation at the bottom is understood as directly connected to the profits at the top, and as a problem of distribution, rather than an inevitable outcome of outsourcing, it becomes harder to justify. Just as the deadly Triangle fire was a preventable and unnecessary outcome of an asymmetric power relationship, the Rana Plaza disaster was the outcome of a global business system designed to put governments and businesses from the poorest countries in ruthless competition with each other for Western business.

If we allow the excuse that "a bad job is better than no job," we must accept the extreme power imbalances of modern fashion supply chains as natural and inevitable, rather than see them for what they are: a deliberately designed system of exploitation that should be radically transformed.

THE SEARCH for cheap labor is ongoing. Today, it is leading many brands to a country with no statutory minimum wage for private sector workers: Ethiopia. In 2017, I spent a few weeks in this East African country and, with the support of local research partners, gathered testimonies of over forty garment workers from four factories that

Excessively long hours, sexual harassment, extreme work pressure, and a work climate so hot and dusty that workers frequently collapse at their workstations: the resemblance to the grievances of 1909 is striking. The only way the garment trade will make progress is for workers to find new ways of challenging and correcting the power imbalance that brands and retailers, with the support of political elites, have willfully escalated.

T**HE IRONY** of the Nike Foundation's "empowerment" philanthropy is that true empowerment is exactly what Nike refuses to get behind in its own operations. Its foundation's work is not a generous investment in women's rights, but a smart business investment to restore the company's image. Putting money into their foundation and their communications department, after all, costs them much less than ensuring the women workers get paid a wage high enough to keep their families together. Philanthropic campaigns and "Corporate Social Responsibility" initiatives serve to fix the disjuncture between the

global stage, should no longer look away. Instead, we should look for new strategies to correct the power imbalances responsible for the unnecessary exploitation and deadly accidents in the factories where our sneakers and T-shirts are made. That means using our power as voters and consumers to demand new kinds of trade deals – trade deals that require strong labor rights and living wages. As Clara Lemlich, tired of discussion over whether or not to strike, said: "I am a working girl. One of those who are on strike against intolerable conditions. I am tired of listening to speakers who talk in general terms. What we are here for is to decide whether we shall strike or shall not strike. I offer a resolution that a general strike be declared now."

Humane hours? Crazy. A living wage? Crazy. Freedom from harassment and humiliation? Crazy. Maternity leave? Crazy. Collective bargaining power and the right to strike? Crazy, crazy, crazy, crazy, and crazy.

> that
> etter
> still
> **invoked to justify the conditions under which products and profits are made.**

Not So Simple

Notes from a Tech-Free Life

MARK BOYLE

Who hasn't dreamed of living a more wholesome, less frenetic life? Ten years ago economist Mark Boyle tried living without money. Two years ago he foreswore modern technology as well. We asked him what he's learned since he ditched his stupidphone and logged off antisocial media.

Around eleven p.m. the night before the winter solstice of 2016 I unplugged my laptop and turned off my phone for what I hoped would be forever. I had just put the finishing touches to a straw-bale cabin that I'd spent the summer building on the three-acre, half-wild smallholding where I live. The following morning I intended to begin a new life without modern technology. There would be no running water, no fossil fuels, no clock, no electricity or any of the things it powers: no washing machine, internet, phone, radio, or light bulb. I was not under the illusion that it was going to be a romantic, bucolic idyll, as it is sometimes portrayed to be. For one, I planned to live directly from the landscape around me without chainsaw, power tools, or tractor.

Mark Boyle writes for the Guardian *and is the author of* The Way Home: Tales from a Life without Technology *(Oneworld, 2019), on which this article is based. He lives in Ireland.*

I woke up the next morning with mixed feelings. On the one hand I felt that sense of liberation that comes from paring things back to the raw ingredients of life, and no longer having bills; on the other, that sense of apprehension that comes with giving up everything you've ever known, in effect burning your bridges to modernity. Right then I had no idea if unplugging from the industrial world would mean I'd lose all touch with reality, or finally discover it.

Living without Money

Eight years earlier I had begun living without money in what was originally intended to be a one year experiment into what anthropologists call "gift culture." I wanted to see if it were possible and, if it were, what it looked and felt like. This hadn't been a light-hearted decision. With a background in economics and business, I came to the sobering conclusion that at the heart of our ecological, geopolitical, social, and cultural malaise was our extreme disconnection from the sources of what we consume. Money, I reasoned, allowed us to never have to come eye-to-eye with the consequences of our consumerist ways. The wider the degrees of separation, the more room for abuse.

> **Would unplugging from the industrial world mean I'd lose all touch with reality, or finally discover it?**

But while renouncing money certainly helped me extricate myself from the jaws of rapacious capitalism, I hadn't escaped industrialism. At the time I used solar panels, which powered some of the things only monetary, industrialized economies can provide: LEDs, a laptop, and gadgets of all sorts. I grew uncomfortable with this and slowly came to feel that it wasn't just monetary economics and capitalism at the heart of the convergence of crises facing us. It was also industrialism.

I don't write much these days about the reasons I have unplugged myself from industrial civilization. This is in part because, deep down, we know them too well already, and it's not for want of information that we continue down that path. I could name a few: the mass extinction of species; resource wars; cultural imperialism; climate catastrophe; widespread surveillance; standardization; the colonization of wilderness and indigenous lands; the fragmentation of community; the automation of millions of jobs with the inevitable inequality, unemployment, and purposelessness that ensue (providing fertile ground for demagogues to take control); the stark decline in mental health; the rise in industrial-scale illnesses such as cancer, heart disease, diabetes, depression, autoimmune diseases and obesity; the tyranny of fast-paced, relentless communication; and the addictiveness of the hollow excitement (films, pornography, TV series, new products, celebrity gossip, dating websites, 24/7 news) that exists behind our screens, the goal of which seems to be the monetization of our distraction.

These concerns all still matter immensely. Yet, surprisingly, over time I found my reasons slowly change. They now have less to do with saving the world, and much more to do with savoring the world. The world needs savoring.

Bare Bones

I wanted to put my finger on the pulse of life again. I wanted to feel the elements in their enormity, to strip away the nonsense and lick the bare bones of existence clean. I wanted to know intimacy, friendship, and community, and not just the things that pass for them. Instead of spending my life making a living, I wanted to make living my life.

Most of all, I wanted to be an animal, to be fully human. I wanted to feel cold and hunger and fear. I wanted to live, not merely exhibit the signs of life, and when the time came, to be ready to go off into the woods, calmly and clearly, and let the life there feed on my flesh, just as I had done on theirs. Crows eating out my eyes, a fox gnawing at my face, a feral dog chewing on my bones, a pine marten making good use of my leg meat. It only seemed fair.

At this point you're probably thinking that here is someone with acute masochistic tendencies. I could hardly blame you. Strangely, the opposite is closer to the truth. Words like "giving up," "living without," and "quitting" are always in danger of sounding limiting and austere, drawing attention to the loss instead of what might be gained. Alcoholics are more likely to be described as "giving up the booze" than "gaining good health and relationships." In my experience, loss and gain are an ongoing part of all of our lives. Choices are always being made whether we know it or not. Throughout most of my life, for reasons that made perfect sense, I chose money and machines, unconsciously choosing to live without the things they have replaced. The question concerning each of us, then, one we too seldom ask ourselves, is: What are we prepared to lose, and what do we want to gain, as we fumble our way through our short, precious lives?

Complexifying

This way of life I have now adopted is often called "the simple life," but that's entirely misleading. It's actually quite complex, made up of a thousand simple things. By contrast, my old life in the city was quite simple, but made up of a thousand complex things, like smartphones and plug sockets and plastic. The innumerable technologies of industrial civilization are so

complex they make our own lives simple.

Too simple. I, for one, got bored doing the same thing day in, day out, using complex technologies that, I suspected, made those who manufactured them bored too. That's partially why I rejected them. With all the switches, buttons, websites, vehicles, devices, entertainment, apps, power tools, gizmos, service providers, comforts, and conveniences surrounding me, I found there was almost nothing left for me to do for myself; except, that is, to earn money to acquire all these things. So, as Kirkpatrick Sale wrote in *Human Scale,* my wish became "to complexify, not simplify."

Living without running water, electricity, or machines, my life has certainly become more complex. Having no flush toilet, I start the day emptying the composting toilet into one of the

Photograph by Hunter Brumels (public domain)

composting bays, which in eighteen months' time will be used to grow food. From there it's off to the spring to fetch the day's washing and drinking water. Along the way I meet and chat with neighbors. After that it could be any number of things: making cider, hauling logs from the forest, sawing and chopping them by hand, foraging plants and berries, manuring vegetable beds, planting trees, skinning a road-kill pheasant or deer, planting seeds, weeding the herb garden, washing in the lake, whittling a spoon. Or any of a hundred other things modernity had once done for me.

What I think people mean by "the simple life" is the uncomplicated essence of it all, and, yes, there is a timeless simplicity to it. I've found that when you peel off the plastic that industrial civilization vacuum-packs around you, what remains couldn't be simpler. Healthy food. Something to be enthusiastic about. Fresh air. A sense of belonging and aliveness. Good water. Purpose. Intimacy. A vital and deep connection to life. The kind of things I did without for too many years.

Part of our longing is for a deeper sense of connection with other people. When I first decided to quit complex technologies, my biggest concern was that I'd cut myself off from my family, friends, and the rest of society. After all, that society is now organized through smartphones, websites, email, and social media. Yet the opposite has proven true. I now stay in touch with those I care about by letter, the writing of which provokes an entirely different quality of thought and expression than email or text. I've never been more social with my neighbors and those dear to me since giving up social media, and many people come and stay in the free hostel we host on our smallholding. Just as importantly, I've come to value quiet, reflective time with landscape and wildlife as much as time with people.

What I Eat

My relationship to food, and thus the world around me, has changed dramatically. When I lived without money, I was an animal rights activist, and strictly vegan for over a decade. These days I live from the landscape around me. Most dinners consist of the pike or trout I catch, the greens or berries I forage, the potatoes and vegetables and salads I grow, and any roadkill – mostly deer, pheasant, or pigeon – that I come across. It's not to everyone's taste, but I know where my food comes from, I know what it entails, and I've never been more aware that my own life depends upon the intimacy of my connection to this landscape.

That change wasn't easy. I love wildlife, and so I take life with the reluctance of one who needs to eat. But I harm more life in the soil from one morning's gardening than I do in a year's fishing. While I'm as opposed to cruelty as ever, I no longer have a problem with death. Death is life, and nothing exists without it. The problem is scale, and the disconnection it confers. I also felt my previous, so-called vegan life wasn't even vegan. Cars aren't vegan. Phones aren't vegan. Plastic isn't vegan. Tubs of vitamins aren't vegan. Protein bars, chickpeas, soya and hemp seeds – none of it is vegan, not really. It's all the harvest of a political ideology that is causing the sixth mass extinction of species, one that is wiping out one habitat after the next and polluting the world around us, making the Earth uninhabitable for much of life – even ourselves.

Liberation from the Clock

When I quit modern technology, I also wanted to give up time. Obviously not seasonal time and the inescapable natural rhythm of day and night; I mean clock-time. I appreciate that this may sound fanciful, impractical, and odd, but it is at the heart of the way of life I want to lead. Reading Jay Griffiths's deep exploration of time, *Pip Pip*, reinforced in my mind how recent the concept of clock-time is in human culture, and how essentially ideological and political it is. Clock-time is central to industry, mass production, specialized division of labor, economies of scale and standardization – basically everything I am trying to move away from. In her typical poetic prose, Griffiths calls Greenwich Mean Time the "meanest time of all."

As I have no clock, my relationship with time has changed dramatically. Things do take longer. There is no electric kettle to make my tea in three minutes, no supermarket to pop into for bread and pizza. But here's the odd bit: I find myself with more time. Writing with a pencil, I can't get distracted by clickbait or advertising. Life has a more relaxed pace, with less stress. I feel in tune not only with seasonal rhythms but also with my own body's rhythm. Instead of an alarm clock, I wake up to the sounds of birds, and I've never slept better. If I want to drop everything and go hiking, I can. I am finally learning to "be here now." There's more diversity, less repetition. Mindfulness is no longer a spiritual luxury, but an economic necessity. While this may not be the most profitable career path, it's good for my own bottom line: happiness.

Romanticizing Simplicity?

Not everything has been easy – far from it. With no phone, there's no more calling faraway family and friends, no text message to meet a mate at the pub. Washing crouched in an aluminum tub with a jug of water is as unromantic as it sounds. But I've learned that this way of life has its own pattern, with old, forgotten solutions. Instead of getting endless emails, text messages, and calls, I receive one or two letters a day, and these matter to me. Eventually I built an outdoor hot tub, and soaking under the stars with a glass of homemade blackberry wine is as romantic as it sounds.

> **I've never been more social with my neighbors and those dear to me since giving up social media.**

I've found that when you say no to one thing, you are saying yes to another. Take music, for example. The day I rejected the immortalizing world of television, radio, and the internet, it was as if all the world-famous artists I loved died at once. No more Bowie or Joni Mitchell. There's a strange sadness about that. But quitting electronic music prompted me to start going to live traditional music sessions, and I love that now. I'm even learning to play (badly) myself.

I don't romanticize the past. But I don't romanticize the future either. I've lived with tech and without, and I know which one brings me most peace and contentment. Aldo Leopold once said that "we all strive for safety, prosperity, comfort, long life, and dullness." It's all too easy to live a long time without having ever felt alive. In the unceasing tradeoff between comfort and that feeling of being fully alive, for most of my life I was failing to find the right balance. Now I want to feel all of the emotions and elements in their entirety. The rain, the joy, the wonder – all of it. ⟍

The Heart's Necessities

JANE TYSON CLEMENT WITH BECCA STEVENS

WHAT ARE THE HEART'S NECESSITIES? It's a question Jane Tyson Clement (1917–2000) asked herself over and over, both in her poetry and in the way she lived. Her observation of the seasons of the soul and of the natural world have made her poems beloved to many readers, most recently singer-songwriter Becca Stevens, who has given Clement's poetry new life – and a new audience – as lyrics in her songs. This book interweaves Clement's best poems with the story of her life, and with commentary by Stevens describing

Jane Tyson Clement

how specific poems speak to her own life, passions, and creative process.

Several years ago, Becca Stevens was struggling to write a song in honor of a close friend and musical collaborator, Kenya Tillery. By chance, she came across two of Jane Tyson Clement's poems, "Winter" and "Tillery," that had both the perfect theme and the perfect rhythm to match the melody she had already composed. The resulting song, "Tillery," was the first of five new songs, and the beginning of an artistic collaboration that led to a new *Plough* book, *The Heart's Necessities: Life in Poetry*.

The Heart's Necessities
Life in Poetry
Jane Tyson Clement with Becca Stevens
Edited by Veery Huleatt
Softcover • 160 pages • April 2019
plough.com/heartsnecessities

The Patterned Heart

The patterned heart is stubborn to reform;
the soul desires forever its first food
and lives but briefly on a different fare;
the eye accustomed to the edge of earth
battles with hills that shut the edge from view;
the ear that listened first to silences
struggles with sound as a bird within the net.

We are not sand to shift beneath the wind,
showing new contours after every storm;
more than the blast of hate must turn my love,
more than the noise of logic change my faith;
my food was peace, my vision space, my sound
the sound of silence, and by these alone
will I be moved to come into my own.

JULY 5, 1940
PENDLE HILL, PENNSYLVANIA

Bach Invention

If I could live as finished as this phrase,
no note too strong; each cadence purposed, clear,
the logic of the changing harmony
building and breaking to a major chord
strangely at home within a minor web
of music; if I could define my end,
from the beginning measures trace my course,
I might be old and prudent, shown by laws
how to devise a pattern for my days
and still be free, unhampered, yet refined.

He sat before the keys and turned the notes
into a fabric of design and peace;
here are the notes, the keys, my fingers free
to run them through their course, and here my mind
seeing his wisdom work within the chords,
finding his knowledge in the finished line.
I would be wise if such restraint were mine.

1939
SMITH COLLEGE, MASSACHUSETTS

Becca Stevens:

I stand behind every word of this poem! Bach's music takes my breath away, gathers my focus with its dancing lines, and inspires me with its intricacy, confidence, and sensitivity. Three centuries after his death, Bach's voice is still like no other, and his music is as inspiring as the day he first "sat before the keys and turned the notes / into a fabric of design and peace."

Bach is my desert island composer. His compositions are spiritual, perfect, complex yet direct, meditative, and, even after thousands of listens, they never cease to reveal something new. I love Jane's idea of life like a Bach phrase, "no note too strong; each cadence purposed, clear . . . at home within a minor web," embodying the balance of restraint and freedom in Bach's writing.

I picture a twenty-two-year-old Jane at the piano, playing through a Bach invention,

Becca Stevens

moved to peace and poetic inspiration by the musical fabric, and admiring the restraint and maturity with which it was woven.

I relate to Jane's sentiment here: "I would be wise if such restraint were mine," especially when I read her poetry. Jane exemplifies that restraint, but the fact that she doesn't recognize it in herself makes her that much more beautiful as an artist, always reaching and seeing her own potential beyond her grasp.

Soli Deo Gloria means "To God alone be the glory." Bach sometimes put the initials SDG at the end of his works to indicate where the attention should be. While the Goldberg Variations were not church music, they touch me, as does all of Bach's music, on a divine and spiritual level, as if the music is a connection between human listeners and God.

Above, and following spread: Bay Head, New Jersey, near Jane Tyson Clement's childhood summer home

---

Brooklyn-based singer-songwriter Becca Stevens has been hailed for her unique ability to craft exquisite compositions, drawing upon elements of pop, indie-rock, jazz, and traditional Appalachian folk. Her albums include Regina *(2017), and* Imperfect Animal *(2015).*

Out of a Difficult and Troubled Season

Out of a difficult and troubled season
the timely harvest thrusts amid the stones;
the dry mind that would claim a thousand reasons
melts beneath the Lord's appointed rain.

The furred magnolia buds we bring to warmth
here in the heated room soon bloom and sicken;
the tree without keeps its own secret time.

Powerless are we to move God with our clamor,
to seize the least fringe of His mystery;
but we must wait until the gift is given
and poor, walk faithfully the lanes of heaven.

OCTOBER 1954 – JUNE 1955
WOODCREST, NEW YORK

Who Owns a River?

CHRISTIAN WOODARD

Five Hundred Miles by Raft with a Floating Colony of Friends

F ROM WHERE I sculled in the flatwater above rapids called, ominously, the Big Drops, I watched the rafts ahead of me – first one, then another, then a third – hit a big breaking wave and flip. I had heard that river guides called the wave Satan's Gut. Or, more fitting, given that I was at the end of a month-long river trip before my wedding: the Mother-in-Law.

The Green River, like nearly every other American desert river, is dammed for irrigation, electricity production, and water storage. For five hundred miles, though, it flows unchecked from the north to the south of Utah. From Flaming Gorge Dam, the river cuts through the Uinta Mountains, curves into Colorado and back to Utah, bisects the Tavaputs Plateau, threads the three volcanic ranges of southern Utah – the La Sals, Abajos, and Henrys – and finally becomes Lake Powell on the border of Arizona. It is the country's longest undammed wilderness waterway outside of Alaska, and in March 2017, a group of friends and I set out to row the whole thing.

While the water flows freely, the adjacent lands are broken into parcels, and the river's uses are decided by whoever owns the surrounding land: wildlife refuges and management areas, the Bureau of Land Management (BLM), national recreation areas, Dinosaur National Monument, Canyonlands National Park, and native reservations. These managers each treat the river differently – as a national treasure, irrigation source, and sewage disposal, to name a few of its uses.

Because each agency issues permits only for its own section, running the whole Green is not as simple as driving to the put-in and shoving off. Occasionally, people row long stretches of the river, but we personally knew only one who went the whole way: Ken Sleight, the model for one of the characters in Edward Abbey's *The*

Below the Gates of Lodore. Photographs by Kari Nielsen.

Christian Woodard is a writer and wilderness guide based in Laramie, Wyoming.

the way Americans practiced it. If the Land Office (predecessor of today's Bureau of Land Management) distributed its customary square sections, a few barons would control all the water. He suggested, instead, parcels based on topography, allowing each claimant access to surface water. He even proposed that political boundaries nest inside watersheds, so that each state, county, town, and "colony" – Powell's preferred term for the kind of cooperative settlements he recommended – administered its own water resources.

Then, as now, Powell's recommendation sounded like a fringe, anti-progress delusion. The Land Office listened politely to his advice, but went on to survey the dry, mountainous region as if it were Iowa. A century and a half later, we have dammed and diverted not just the Green but most Western rivers to develop desert cities. Instead of the communal sensibilities Powell advised, we have chosen intricate compacts and trades, incapable of apportioning a shrinking water supply. People are ready to fight for their water, their cultural heritage, and their square property lines.

LIKE POWELL, I was raised in western New York in a Wesleyan family. Long before seeing the American Southwest, I had read about the Semitic tribes of Genesis, who traveled between grass and water. By the time Powell reached the Southwest, some white herders were living a similar, semi-nomadic life. He described them in his 1878 *Report on the Lands of the Arid Region of the United States:*

Melake and Eyal share Ethiopian Lent food.

"people who are already in the country and who have herds with which they roam about seeking water and grass, and making no permanent residences."

These people had left civilization's captivity to return to transient, subsistence life – like the Hebrews of the Exodus, whose "wandering in the wilderness" is recorded in Numbers 33 as a series of points linked by travel. It is a curvi-linear journey through which the Hebrews mold themselves to the demands of the land and cement their tribal society. One example reads: "They set out from Marah and came to Elim; at Elim there were twelve springs of water and seventy palm trees, and they camped there. And they set out from Elim and camped by the Red Sea. And they set out from the Red Sea and camped in the wilderness of Sin."

It sounds a lot like a log of our river trip: "Camped in Brown's Park. Found a dead elk tangled in barbed wire around a Wilderness Study Area. Left Brown's Park. Rowed toward the Uintas, camped on river left." It is also characteristic of Mormon pioneer journals, and of the patterns of overlapping indigenous groups who lived along the Green before its division into refuges and reservations, monuments and parks. One of our friends on the trip, a cartographer, calls accounts like this "networks" – a way of conceptualizing land that prioritizes movement and answers the question *How do I get there from here?*

Yet if the American desert was to be made a Promised Land, as the Mormons and the Land Office both envisioned in their own ways, it needed a new settlement model. When the Hebrews cross the Jordan into Canaan, they pitch their geographic language in a new way:

When you enter the land of Canaan (this is land that shall fall to you for an inheritance, the land of Canaan, defined by its boundaries), your south sector shall extend from the

wilderness of Zin along the side of Edom. Your southern boundary shall begin from the end of the Dead Sea on the east; your boundary shall turn south of the ascent of Akrabbim. . . .

And so on for eight verses until the region has been outlined with an imaginary surveyor's transit: ". . . and its end shall be at the Dead Sea. This shall be your land with its boundaries all around." The land is no longer linked by pathways; it is divided into parcels. A map like this prioritizes permanence and resource use, and answers the question *Who owns what?*

Network maps – of rivers, trails, or stars – show up in non-agrarian societies, whether they hunt, fish, herd, or gather for subsistence. Property maps belong to settled, agrarian societies.

For the first explorers of the interior West and their indigenous forebears, the land's aridity, soil, grade, and aspect were ultimate authorities. But the link between human and natural systems was broken by the same thinking that treated the Jordan as an edge instead of the heart of a valley. After one hundred and fifty years of agrarian experimentation in the arid region, the networks are all but buried under legalities and property boundaries. On our trip, we hoped to find hints of the lost pathways, letting our habits grow with the requirements of the river.

WHILE MANY river-runners have dreamed of a long Green River trip, the journey was especially significant for Kari and me. One of our first dates had been a canoe trip on the Green. A few years later, I had proposed to her in a slot canyon near the river. We had made some of our best friends on different sections of the Green, and connecting the whole river would bring us and our friends together for the wedding.

On March 15, 2017, a little less than one hundred and fifty years after Powell started his expedition, six of us packed boats at Flaming Gorge Dam, near the Wyoming border. Kari's sister, Lindsey, stowed bags of dried food with her best friend, Rachel. Ryann, a raft guide who had helped Ken Sleight edit his memoirs, pumped the raft tubes. Kari adjusted the canoe's sprayskirt with Pete, a biologist from Salt Lake. I chatted with some fishermen.

Most of us had been down the Grand Canyon or other parts of the watershed together. Ten years earlier, Pete and I had retraced a historic canoe route across Nunavut. Lindsey and Rachel had been kayak guides in Southeast Alaska and Baja. We were all familiar enough with long trips to respect the moment of shoving off. We had planned everything carefully, but once we were underway the rendezvous points, food drops, and shuttles

Ryann Savino pulls into the Uinta Basin.

would be set in stone. Untying the boats meant committing to bring everyone through safely and to arrive on time, not only at each of the four bridges that cross the Green on its five-hundred-mile descent, but to our own wedding, exactly one month away. Snow hung on the shady ridges, and Flaming Gorge Dam released two thousand cubic feet per second of clear, green water, headed for Lake Powell. We bobbed at the end of the ropes for a minute, then cast off into the current.

The trip's first addition came three days later, at the Dinosaur National Monument checkpoint. We traded Pete for Eyal, who had taken his first raft trip with Kari and me less than a year before. He had loved all of it – whitewater, long conversations, good food, and the rhythm of waking up each morning on the river. He had signed on for our Green River trip without hesitation, excited to row every rapid despite his inexperience. Others would come and go at each bridge, but the six of us would make the whole rest of the trip. We grilled dinner and watched the river pour into a quartzite hallway that Powell's group had named the Gates of Lodore.

Twenty days in, it was feeling normal to wake up covered in sand.

In 1966, the Bureau of Reclamation proposed a project to flood the Gates of Lodore. The Sierra Club and Wilderness Society, arguing that national monuments should be exempt from development, successfully opposed the plan. Partially because of that precedent, modern developers are wary of new monument designations.

In the morning, a ranger equipped with a bulletproof vest, pistol, Taser, pepper spray, and very thorough checklist met us at the rafts. Eyal, who has both a congenital and a conditioned distrust of law enforcement, retreated to the farthest raft and crossed his arms. The ranger asked what we planned to do with our poop. We told him we would pack it out in ammo cans.

He asked what day we intended to pass the Yampa confluence, the only other road access inside Dinosaur National Monument. We told him March 20.

He asked how many pulleys we had. None. No, maybe two? Carabiners work fine. How many are we supposed to have?

He was just checking. They were not required. Have a nice trip.

Eyal shoved us off with slightly more gusto than necessary. We rowed into the Gates, where Powell's expedition had pinned a boat on a rock. Maybe if they had had pulleys, they could have saved it.

Three days later, we floated under the towering, overhung fin of Weber sandstone that marks the Yampa confluence. The same ranger stood on the beach, hands on his gun belt, elbows out. I waved, Eyal scowled, and the ranger shook his head ambiguously. We kept on through Whirlpool and Split Mountain Canyons, stopping to soak in a tepid hot spring.

We floated out of Dinosaur and the high, snowbound Uinta plateau came into relief. We were entering the forgotten heart of the Green: the Uinta Basin. Surrounded by a patchwork of private and state land, a wildlife refuge, and fragments of Uintah and Ouray Reservation, it sees less attention from scientists and land managers than any other section of the river. While seventeen thousand people float through Dinosaur every year, the hundred miles of flatwater just downstream are nearly deserted.

Ironically, when Powell set out, the Uinta Basin was the only mapped section of the river. Soon after he pushed off, his expedition was rumored lost, and settlers in the basin watched for broken boats and bodies. A month later, Powell's group coasted into known territory, where they sent letters home, resupplied (per their congressional mandate) at the only Army post they would encounter, and got sick on potato greens from a homesteader's garden. It was to be their last taste of civilization until they emerged from the Grand Canyon three months later.

In the intervening century and a half, the known and unknown territories of the Green have exactly reversed. The wild water and inescapable walls that intimidated Powell's men have become the river-runner's back yard. Many river guides have spent their careers on the Green without dipping an oar in the Uinta Basin.

So as we floated south we felt some of the exploratory thrill that charged Powell's trip. There were no new canyons to name but everything sparkled under the light of discovery. Ryann pulled over to pee and found a goose nest with six eggs. Lindsey drew cranes and pelicans wheeling over freshly planted fields. We collected driftwood and willows and made our campfires where the cows came down to drink. We fought headwinds and pushed through miles of deadwater, thick with fertilizer foam. One afternoon we passed a bluff covered in cowboy petroglyphs – brands and spurs, horses and names pecked into the rock. We slept under crackling high-tension lines, and with the hinge and beat of scattered oil rigs.

Just upstream of the Ouray bridge, we picked up another friend and slept across the road from a pumping station. At intervals, tanker trucks geared down into the lot, took on river water, and went back out into the night.

FROM SAND WASH, where the Tavaputs Plateau rises around the river in gray cliffs, the Green flows through Desolation and Gray Canyons, eighty-three miles of easy whitewater. We checked in with the Bureau of Land Management, which oversees the right bank of the river, and verified our permit to camp on Ute land, river left.

While the tribe and the BLM hold the majority of the land on the Tavaputs, there are a few private inholdings, including the Rock Creek Ranch, homesteaded in 1914 but now falling to ruin. When we pulled up, the unpruned apple and apricot trees were blooming, and Rock Creek poured snowmelt into the river. Roofless sandstone buildings held relics too heavy or useless to lug back to civilization – a cast-iron stove, a weather-curled boot, some carefully stacked patches of window screen.

Wild goose nest

Powell's 1878 report suggested that groups of settlers could share these fertile bottomlands, supporting each other through the inevitable droughts, hard winters, and remoteness of high desert homesteading. "The pasturage farms cannot be fenced – they must be occupied in common," he said. "These lands could be settled and improved by the 'colony' plan better than by any other. . . . Customs are forming and regulations are being made by common consent among the people in some districts already." The setting, he thought, demanded cooperation and communal accountability.

America, though, was high on individualism, technological progress, and frontier optimism. Claimants like the Rock Creek Ranch staked springs and streams controlling thousands of surrounding acres, fenced out competitors, and shortly went bankrupt. Some unwanted land was allotted to native groups, and the Bureau of Land Management got the rest. Today, the BLM manages over two-thirds of Utah's land.

Into this landscape, which Wallace Stegner called "the most spectacular and humanly the least usable of all our regions," we brought our own small colony. By that point, Lindsey had used up a handful of pens on her daily ink drawings. Kari and I had gotten violently ill by eating a cactus. Ryann had read aloud her favorite desert writers over watercress- and nettle-topped pan pizzas. Eyal was teaching us the Hebrew alphabet. We wanted not to "use" the land, but to cultivate a strong community in reference to it. Faith in human wisdom and dignity recognizes those characteristics in the surrounding landscape. It allows natural systems their own power, not as resources, but as home. Twenty days in, it was feeling normal to wake up covered in sand.

I N GREEN RIVER State Park, three hundred miles from our starting point, we ate cinnamon rolls and took long showers. We picked up ten more friends, three rafts, and a whitewater canoe. Ken Sleight and his wife, Jane – and their goat, Rosa – drove from Moab to see us off on the last stretch before our wedding. We planned to float through Labyrinth, Stillwater, and Cataract Canyons, taking out at the Dirty Devil River, where Ken used to start his favorite trips, through Glen Canyon.

In the late 1950s, Ken helped pioneer Glen Canyon rafting. He advertised two-week floats with military surplus rafts, which he carried to the river by

Fremont petroglyphs, Jones Hole.

mule train. In the old pictures, he's a skinny man with big ears and a big smile. A caricature of that young river guide became "Seldom Seen Smith" in *The Monkey Wrench Gang*, Edward Abbey's 1975 novel of sabotage and environmental protest. Seldom Seen is an elusive, fiery character, equally at home on a river trip or obstructing land development. He cuts fence and disables machinery. He has forsaken Mormonism, but still prays. In one scene he kneels on Glen Canyon Dam, beseeching the Lord to destroy the offending structure with a "precision-type earthquake."

Ken, also raised Mormon, has protested the dam from the beginning, founding several eco-defense groups and successfully suing the federal government in 1970. He has been a fervent voice in southwestern water and environmental debates. Despite Ken's similarities to Seldom Seen, Abbey never identified his longtime friend as the character's model.

Now eighty-eight, Ken still has the big smile, and slightly bigger ears. More than fifty years after the Bureau of Reclamation flooded Glen Canyon and rebranded it Lake Powell, after its first surveyor, Ken still calls it "Lake Foul." Ken asked us if the Uinta Basin had been windy. It had. He nodded. It's always windy up there. He tapped on Ryann's raft, checking the tubes for pressure. He nodded again, and wished us luck in Cataract. We all watched Rosa the goat poke her nose into the river and snatch it back.

The water was brown and cold. Spring melt was coming into its own, and below the Colorado confluence the river was forecast to reach thirty-five thousand cubic feet per second. In high water, Cataract is one of the most difficult sections of the river. Even the Grand Canyon, just downstream but now regulated by Glen Canyon Dam, rarely equals its volume and gradient.

Ken and Jane – and Rosa the goat – headed back to Moab, and we pushed off for the smooth sandstone of Canyonlands National Park. It would take us another week to follow the river into deeply cut dune formations, then through delta deposits with chunks of petrified wood, the hard White Rim, a series of sandstones and shales, and after the confluence with the Colorado, into the faulted complex of shallow sea sediments that form Cataract Canyon's whitewater.

We camped downstream from the confluence on a broad sand bench, circled by clifftop needles and spires. The last sunlight came through the rocks and a nearly full moon rose across the river. Far upstream, we heard the voices of our final group of friends, rowing down the Colorado to meet us. From the original group of six, we had grown to twenty-one boisterous friends, happy to be back on the water together.

The next day we all climbed to the rim to see Cataract's first rapids roll around a corner. Past that bend, the river makes the western boundary of the Abajo Mountains, Dark Canyon, and Cedar Mesa, now under review as federal officials debate the future of the vast Bears Ears National Monument. The granaries and dwellings in those cliffs have been inhabited, abandoned, and re-inhabited for five thousand years. Clovis points from the area could be more than twice as old.

The fight over Bears Ears involves questions about whether the cultural history and the natural integrity of land within the monument are compatible with cattle ranching, oil and gas extraction, and the high-volume tourism that land protection invites. But these cultural and eco-regions stretch beyond Bears Ears into the plateau's headwaters – southern Wyoming, western Colorado, and northern Arizona and New Mexico. We had seen pictographs and

petroglyphs from the very top of our journey, and if the man-made Lake Powell had not covered them with its water, we would have seen more downstream. The entire Colorado Plateau is linked by its waterways and the traditional routes of its inhabitants.

Should we protect Bears Ears? Should we regret flooding Glen Canyon or saving Dinosaur? Can we accept our role in transforming a once-living landscape into a set of resources to be exploited? These questions are inevitably political. But they are spiritual and moral, too, no matter how ill-equipped we are to recognize and discuss them in that way.

It is impossible to know whether Powell would have approved of the extractive morality that his surveys enabled. He certainly would not have been surprised. After his shoestring first descent, Powell returned to the Green and Colorado Rivers for a government-funded survey in 1871 to 1872. His maps became the basis for the fledgling United States Geological Survey, which he directed for more than a decade.

In 1879, frustrated by the Land Office's disregard for his recommendations for limited, communal settlement of the arid region, Powell tried a new tack. With the Smithsonian's support, he founded the Bureau of American Ethnology to research native languages and traditions that the surveys had

Kari, Melake, and Eyal near the end of Gray Canyon. Photograph by Christian Woodard.

Storm in
Rainbow Park

already begun to displace. After a career in empirical, physical geography, Powell came to believe that the land we inhabit is shaped by the stories we tell.

It has taken more than a century of development, but interest is growing in Powell's ethnographic work and its embedded, land-centric morality. Of course, our inherited stories are not going away: Moses taking off his sandals, or striking water from the rock. The straight-line boundaries of the Promised Land. Ken Sleight, rowing through Glen Canyon's smooth meanders for the last time. Little by little, we are finding ways to integrate those stories and add some of our own – from a first date to a complete descent with a floating colony, preparing for our wedding by living closely with the river.

W E S P E N T the day on the rim, climbing strange rocks. In the afternoon, we came down to help Eyal prepare a Passover seder. We collected bitter herbs and kept a fire under the lamb. By now, we were all familiar with the currents of one another's moods and gestures. We stayed up late discussing our wanderings, drinking wine, and watching the moon cross from one rim to the other. Like Powell, we had come to believe in self-organizing systems, in which respect for community and for the continuity of the land can reinforce one another.

The next morning, I looked down the tongue of the Big Drop to see three rafts upside down in the foam. Just when things seemed most in hand, we were still at the mercy of the water. I dipped my oars to face the rising wave, and rowed. ⟩

Comrade Ruskin

How a Victorian visionary can save communism from Marx

EUGENE McCARRAHER

hose is the Wealth of the World but yours?" Thus did a radical firebrand address Britain's industrial working class in the summer of 1880, urging them to seize the fruits of their labor: "Do you mean to go on for ever, leaving your wealth to be consumed by the idle, and your virtue to be mocked by the vile? The wealth of the world is yours; even your common rant and rabble of economists tell you that – 'no wealth without industry.' Who robs you of it, then, or beguiles you?"

The militant who penned these words was not Karl Marx, though he was then in London working on the last two volumes of *Capital*. Instead it was a self-professed "violent Tory of the old school" who held the post of Slade Professor of Fine Art at Oxford. His name was John Ruskin.

John Ruskin
in 1863

Ruskin had been writing open letters to "the Workmen and Labourers of Great Britain" since the early 1870s. He titled these missives, somewhat enigmatically, *Fors Clavigera*, or "Fortune the Nail-bearer." They covered an array of subjects: work, property, politics, and art. Addressing the working class as "My Friends" at the beginning of every epistle, he avowed his old-school Toryism in the tenth letter, proudly declaring "a most sincere love of kings, and a dislike of everybody who attempted to disobey them."

Yet two months earlier, in a previous letter, the lover of monarchs and hater of rebels had proclaimed himself a "communist," one who was "reddest also of the red." To be sure, Ruskin used the word *communist* in a sense very different from the one it would carry after the Russian Revolution. In 1871, alarmed by (false) reports that the insurgents of the Paris Commune had destroyed many of the city's churches and monuments, he rejected what he called "the Parisian notion of communism" – the belief that all property should be common property. Instead, he wrote, "we Communists of the old school think that our property belongs to everybody, and everybody's property to us." Therefore even "private" property was common in some way (one that Ruskin, alas, didn't specify). Moreover, he believed that "everybody must work in common, and do common or simple work for his dinner."

Ruskin scholars generally pass over this communism as incoherent or ironic. But I want to argue that it was neither. Instead, it represents a road not taken in the history of movements for a just social order. Today, amid renewed outrage over the depredations of globalized capitalism, it's high time to rediscover Ruskin's vision for how people should live and work together.

Like Marx and other communists of the nineteenth century, Ruskin was addressing some of the most intractable dilemmas of capitalist modernity. These included the expansion of industrial production at the expense of individual control and creativity, an enormous increase in wealth and productivity alongside poverty and despoliation, and an ideal of limitless technological progress that threatened to reduce the heritage of the past to oblivion. They also reflected a new, money-defined view of what it means to be human, one in which men and women are no longer valued as images of God but rather as sources of profitability and efficiency.

Marx believed that the resolution of these conflicts lay in the harsh but ultimately liberating trajectory of capitalism itself, whose own internal contradictions would necessarily goad the proletariat into revolution. (This is the deterministic notion at the heart of so-called scientific socialism.) By contrast, Ruskin rooted his opposition to the tyranny of mammon in a sacramental humanism that was emphatically Christian. For Marx, communism would be the tragicomic endpoint of capitalist development. But for Ruskin, communism represented "the Economy of Heaven": a society that would recover the artisanal mastery destroyed by mechanization and would elide the distinction between private property and the common good. With the freely creative person at its center, Ruskin's kind of communism was to be a political economy of love.

Previous page: William Morris, design for an 1892 edition of John Ruskin's *The Nature of Gothic*

Opposite: William Morris, *Strawberry Thief,* printed textile, 1883

Eugene McCarraher is associate professor of humanities at Villanova University. His second book, The Enchantments of Mammon: How Capitalism Became the Religion of Modernity, *will be published in November by the Belknap Press of Harvard University Press.*

The Un-Convert

Like so many other scourges of the bourgeoisie, Ruskin grew up in a bourgeois family. His father, John James, was a successful wine merchant who was fond of Romantic writers, especially Lord Byron and Sir Walter Scott. His mother, Margaret, was a rigorous evangelical who insisted on his memorizing large parts of the Bible. Thanks to his father's lucrative business, Ruskin had the leisure to read and travel widely. Apart from scripture, he immersed himself in Homer, Shakespeare, Gibbon, and Bunyan, and he visited Scotland, France, Belgium, Germany, and Italy before he was fifteen. Enthralled by the paintings of J. M. W. Turner, young John also took to drawing and writing about nature, filling notebooks with sketches and publishing his first articles on art before he was twenty.

Despite his strict evangelical home and outwardly pious demeanor, Ruskin doubted the faith early on: his devotion "was never strong," he once told a friend, and in his autobiography he confessed that, at age fourteen, he had mused that while angels might have visited Abraham, "none had ever appeared to me that I knew of." He lived with this ambivalence while a student at Oxford. Over the 1840s and 1850s, as his intellectual career accelerated, Ruskin slowly sloughed off the faith of his upbringing, becoming, as he put it, "a conclusively un-converted man."

Yet Ruskin's "un-conversion" was from evangelicalism, not from Christianity. His evolution from art critic to political economist – or rather, his blend of the two vocations – marked an effort to pursue the traditional calling of the prophet in modern times. Like many other Victorian intellectuals, Ruskin was shaken by discoveries in geology, biology, and the historical criticism of the Bible. Some of his contemporaries – Herbert

About the artist: The British philosopher and designer William Morris (1834–1896), a leader of the Arts and Crafts movement, was heavily influenced by John Ruskin. In 1892, Morris's Kelmscott Press issued a hand-printed edition of John Ruskin's *The Nature of Gothic*, a work that came to be a manifesto for the Arts and Crafts movement. The border and illuminated letter on the opening page of this article are taken from that book's first page. Samples of Morris's tapestry designs appear throughout this article.

Spencer, Charles Bradlaugh, T. H. Huxley, George Eliot – embraced secularism, while others – John Henry Newman and the Oxford Movement – affirmed orthodoxy. A third group, which included William Blake, William Wordsworth, and Thomas Carlyle, pioneered a Romantic religiosity that perceived the supernatural within nature: Blake's "heaven in a wild flower" and Wordsworth's "sense sublime / of something far more deeply

William Morris, *Tulip and Willow*, printed textile, 1873

interfused." The Romantics were the modern heirs of the Christian sacramental imagination – the belief that visible, material reality can mediate the grace of God. This was the faith that Ruskin came to embrace.

Conveyed in a Christian idiom, Ruskin's Romanticism surfaced first in his five-volume *Modern Painters* (1843), and then leavened his forays into social criticism and political economy. Artists such as J. M. W. Turner, he asserted in volume one, perceive in nature "that faultless, ceaseless, inconceivable, inexhaustible loveliness, which God has stamped upon all things." Beauty, he wrote in the second volume (1846), "whether [it] occur in a stone, flower, beast, or in man . . . may be shown to be in some sort typical of the Divine attributes." "In the midst of the material nearness of these heavens," he declared in volume four (1856), we "acknowledge His own immediate presence." Because Ruskin saw the sacred in nature, he saw it in humankind as well. "The direct manifestation of Deity to man is in His own image, that is, in man," he wrote in volume five (1860). "The soul of man is a mirror of the mind of God" – a mirror, he rued, "dark distorted, and broken."

Work and Workers

The broken mirror of human divinity was most evident, for Ruskin, in the industrial division of labor. As a host of historians has explained, the Industrial Revolution that commenced in the mid-eighteenth century was a social process as well as a technological one. Driven by the capitalist imperative to lower costs and increase profits, manufacturers realized that they needed to master the production process itself. Succumbing to competition from the early industrialists, artisans and craftsmen who controlled their own tools were dispossessed from the means of production and transformed into wage laborers in factories – "proletarians," in Marxist terms. Now that the link between workers and their tools was broken, labor could be "degraded," rationalized, and broken down into discrete elements – and then relocated from humans to machinery. In this way, the industrial division of labor eroded artisanal skill by mechanizing or automating production. The factory embodied capital's power over the minds and movements of workers. To early industrialists, this was part of the point. In the words of Andrew Ure, who in 1835 wrote one of the first texts on industrial management, factory work would not only enhance profits and productivity but also "restore order among the industrious classes" and "strangle the Hydra of misrule" (*The Philosophy of Manufactures*).

Early critics of industrial capitalism objected at least as much to dispossession and degradation as they did to poverty and misery. Already in the Luddite uprisings in the 1810s, hundreds of weavers in Nottingham and Yorkshire smashed textile machinery as a protest against mechanization. Around the same time, utopian socialists such as Charles Fourier lamented the elimination of play and creativity from work – the logical culmination of industrial labor, the literal de-humanization of production.

The young Marx analyzed the dehumanizing effects of industrialization in some of his writings of the mid-1840s. The essence of humanity, he contended, was "free, conscious activity," a versatile and even artisanal creativity that "forms things in accordance with the laws of beauty." If I create "in a human manner," Marx writes, I make something that bears the mark of "my individuality and its peculiarity"; I delight in satisfying your need, and my personality is "confirmed both in your thought and your love"; I realize "my own essence, my human, my communal essence." The ultimate aim of work is not just production, but the flourishing of a good human life.

Capitalism renders such flourishing impossible by "alienating" the worker from his essence. Alienation is, for Marx, not primarily a psychological malady but rather a social and material deprivation. Because the capitalist owns and controls the means of production – which is to say, for Marx, the means of humanity – he takes for himself not only the wealth that the worker produces, but also "the very act of production itself," the worker's mental and manual virtuosity. Alienation is Marx's account of the dispossession and degradation of craftsmanship that the capitalist achieves through the industrial division of labor.

But because Marx believed in "progress" through the dialectical unfolding of history, alienation was, in his view, a progressive step toward the destination of communism. Because it enabled technological innovation and generated material abundance, the arduous and often violent process of proletarianization was, Marx insisted, historically necessary and beneficial. Placing the industrial proletariat on what Hegel had called "the slaughter-bench of history," capitalist automation made martyrs of workers for the sake of a golden future: the communist utopia of abundance, free time, and mechanized emancipation from labor. By the time Marx published the first volume of *Capital* (1867), machinery was for him both a "demon power" and a historical vehicle to the "realm of freedom."

While Ruskin, like the young Marx, thought of human work in artisanal terms, his communism stemmed from a very different assessment of the impact of industrialization. This requires some explication. Despite claiming to be a "violent Tory," Ruskin was no reactionary, as many of his critics (then and now) have contended. "I am not one who in the least doubts or disputes the progress of this century in many things useful to mankind," he insisted (*The Two Paths*, 1859). What mattered was how to distinguish "the progress of this century" from regression into barbarism. To Ruskin, the industrial division of labor, far from liberating human beings, constituted their disfigurement and profanation. He argued that mechanization – mandated by the imperative of profit – effected "the degradation of the operative into a machine" (*The Nature of Gothic*). Human beings were ingenious, intrepid, and imperfect; the precision of motion dictated by industrial machinery reduced people to machines themselves. "You must either make a tool of the creature, or a man of him. You cannot make both." If you want pliant, efficient workers, "you must unhumanize them," Ruskin warned – which meant that you must desecrate the image and likeness of divinity.

Wealth and Illth

In 1862, Ruskin wrote his most cogent and controversial work on political economy, a collection of four essays titled *Unto This Last*.

It sketches out the theological groundwork for his Romantic communism. Going further than Carlyle, who called economics "the dismal science," Ruskin refused to even acknowledge economics as a science, likening it to "alchemy, astrology, witchcraft, and other such popular creeds." Economics is untrue, not just dismal, he maintained, because it got human nature wrong: a human being is not a rational utility-maximizing calculator but rather "an engine whose motive power is a Soul." Because its starting point was false, economics was like "a science of gymnastics which assumed that men had no skeletons." As with human beings, so with the rest of the world: everything "reaches yet into the infinite," Ruskin mused, and the earth resonates with "amazement" – a measureless, inexhaustible wonder at what Gerard Manley Hopkins would call the grandeur of God.

This keen sense of the sacred in nature and in humankind was the basis for what Ruskin dubbed the "real science" of production and consumption. If the "Soul" was what made us reach yet into the infinite, then true political economy was a science of desire, for "the desire of the heart is also the light of the eyes." The real science of the "Economy of Heaven" taught us how to "desire and labor for the things that lead to life" – life meaning not just survival, but the cultivation of all our powers of "love, of joy, and of admiration." The implication, of course, was that capitalist economics is a science of death – a necro-science that taught us to desire competition, envy, avarice, and corruption. Repudiating these "Laws of Death," Ruskin famously insisted that "there is no wealth but life."

Life as true wealth is the key to understanding Ruskin's distinction between wealth and what he called "illth." Conventional economics measures wealth quantitatively, for example as the tally of goods and services that make up the Gross Domestic Product.

But Ruskin's definition of wealth was qualitative: "the possession of the valuable by the valiant." Such wealth existed in a connection between the nature of a thing and that of its possessor; a valuable object became valueless in the hands of a vicious person. Pursued for the sake of virtue, the true end of wealth was a bounty of "full-breathed, bright-eyed, and happy-hearted human creatures." And since Ruskin favored "great quantity of consumption," he was no ascetic; indeed, consumption, he insisted, is "the final object of political economy."

Yet happy-hearted consumption is far different from what we today call consumerism. Modern consumerism is really a covert culture of production, since profit, not pleasure, is its ultimate goal; its incessant stimulation of desire and dissatisfaction is a means to make money, not to ensure our fulfillment. That is why, for Ruskin, much of capitalist wealth is really "illth": either because it is harmful in itself, or because the value of an object is mismatched to the virtue of its possessor. Such "illth" wreaks "devastation and trouble in all directions" – which is what one would expect from a fraudulent science.

Christian Communism

Ruskin's sacramental economics forms the backdrop for his communism as described in *Fors Clavigera*. While both Ruskin and Marx identified the dislocation of workers from control over production as the fundamental injustice of capitalism, Ruskin's "old-school" communism parted from that of Marx in two significant respects. First, for Marx, communism would be the consummation of a promethean project of industrial development – a project that actually *required* "mammon-service," exploitation, and indignity. For Ruskin, by contrast, communism *defied* the historical necessity of avarice and its industrialized despotism. Second, where Marx emphasized communism as a form of *property* – common ownership – Ruskin emphasized communism as a principle of *morality* – as pre-modern communists had put it well before Marx, "from each according to ability, to each according to need."

The Marxist objection to Ruskin's communism has often been that it idealizes a petty-bourgeois economy of small producers, whose private property relations subvert all their earnest professions of charity. To a Marxist, this is reactionary – capitalist consolidation of the economy is necessary to prepare the way for the collectivization of industry, and eventually, for the communist utopia. (Meanwhile, Ruskin's Christian morality is considered an ideological enemy, blinding workers to the need for revolution.) When it comes to property, the Marxist and the capitalist are thus in agreement: there is either private, capitalist property or common, collectivized property – no other form of property exists. Hence the puzzlement about Ruskin's communism: to Marxists and to capitalists, it's either a disembodied moralism with no effect on the real world, or it's merely an ironic gesture intended to unsettle complacent readers.

But recall Ruskin's shorthand definition of communism: "our property belongs to everybody, and everybody's property to us." What this suggests is a form of property that fudges the distinction between private and collective; indeed, it suggests that private property is never really "private." Anything but ironic, Ruskin's communism forces us to reconsider what we mean by "property" in the first place. As the anthropologist David Graeber reminds us, "property is not really a relation between a person and a thing. It's an understanding or arrangement between people concerning things." (Someone alone on an island, he

William Morris, *Medway*, printed textile, 1885

muses, doesn't worry about property rights.) If property is thus always a social relation, then property is private only because we've all agreed – or been forced to accept – that it should be. So it's perfectly possible to imagine property systems in which what's mine is yours, and what's yours is mine, depending on how we've defined our relationship.

There is a name for a form of social relation in which a person or people can claim rights to objects "owned" by another: usufruct. It's common among archaic and tribal peoples: I own a tool, but if you need it, it's yours as long as you don't damage it. Ownership depends on use; property is a kind of social trust that we'll all use things for the common good. As vehemently as most Christians believe that private (read: capitalist) property is part of the essence of creation, usufruct was a governing principle among ancient and medieval Christian writers. It's there in Luke's account of the early Christians ("No one claimed that any of their possessions was their own, but they shared everything they had"); in Saint Basil's injunction about surplus goods ("The bread that you keep belongs to the hungry, the cloak in your closet to the naked"); and in Saint Thomas Aquinas's argument for the "universal destination of goods."

it marked the end of a Cold War–era skirmish over whether King was a socialist subversive, possibly even a full-blown "Red" who colluded with the Soviet Union.

In the wake of King's assassination, the détente regarding his alleged socialism allowed him to enter the pantheon of American heroes and be ritually celebrated by the state. But the cost of King's canonization was steep, resulting in a narrowed understanding of his ideals and those of the broader civil rights movement.

During King's lifetime, his alleged socialism was an obsession within the American security state, fueled by J. Edgar Hoover, director of the Federal Bureau of Investigation. Hoover, an implacable foe of black political agitation, also used the FBI to undermine figures such as Marcus Garvey, Claudia Jones, W. E. B. Du Bois, and Paul Robeson. The director, admittedly, did not conjure his suspicions about King and communism from thin air. As early as the Montgomery bus boycott (1955–56), King surrounded himself with advisors who had cut their teeth in leftist circles, such as the openly gay socialist and peace activist Bayard Rustin. Worse, from Hoover's point of view, King relied heavily on the fundraising prowess, speechwriting acumen, and intellectual companionship of Stanley Levison, who, as the FBI "warned" King, was also a prolific fundraiser for the Communist Party of the United States of America (CPUSA). That King did not distance himself from Levison at the FBI's behest left Hoover incensed.

Hoover's insistence that King was a communist, or at least a communist dupe, served to justify subjecting him to illegal surveillance, sabotage, and harassment, with the approval of both the Kennedy and Johnson administrations. When field agents reported no clear-cut

J. Edgar Hoover

evidence of King's communism, Hoover ordered them to look harder. As good bureaucrats, they duly manufactured the desired results. After being berated by Hoover, William C. Sullivan, the head of the Domestic Intelligence Division, delivered this infamous assessment of the 1963 March on Washington: "I believe in the light of King's powerful demagogic speech yesterday he stands head and shoulders over all other Negro leaders put together when it comes to influencing great masses of Negroes. We must mark him now, if we have not done so before, as the most dangerous Negro of the future in this Nation from the standpoint of communism, the Negro and national security."

The irony is that, in the end, King likely made more impact on Levison and the communist movement than vice versa. While the FBI could not imagine black intellectuals influencing white ones, it seems that the closer Levison grew to King, the more disillusioned he became with official communism and the CPUSA. King and the surging civil rights revolution became the locus of his hopes for the politics of emancipation.

Though the FBI's surveillance of King had been initiated as an anti-communist measure, it also reflected Hoover's conviction that King was a moral hypocrite and a sexual "degenerate." Indeed, the FBI investigation came to focus so incessantly on sex that this may be its most lasting legacy. Recent allegations by the journalist David Garrow, drawing on declassified FBI memos, charge that King's indefensible sexism – which I have written about at length elsewhere with the feminist theorist Shatema Threadcraft[*] – had more disturbing manifestations than previously known. Yet, as historians

[*] Shatema Threadcraft and Brandon M. Terry, "Gender Trouble: Manhood, Inclusion, and Justice" in Tommie Shelby and Brandon M. Terry, eds., *To Shape a New World: Essays on the Political Philosophy of Martin Luther King, Jr.* (Cambridge, MA: Harvard University Press, 2018).

like Barbara Ransby have argued, accounts like Garrow's, which rely heavily upon unsourced, unverified, and anonymous FBI agent notations, must be taken with "healthy skepticism." Not only was the FBI often simply inept, but its director and his staff shared a clear mission: to destroy black radicalism.

But was King a "radical" in the socialist sense? Jesse Helms, the legendarily racist North Carolina Republican, certainly thought so. In 1983, during the debate to establish a federal holiday in King's memory, Helms denounced him on the Senate floor as an adherent to the "official policy of communism" and "action-oriented Marxism." Helms's words were widely denounced by his Senate colleagues, but President Ronald Reagan's reaction was more oblique. Asked if he thought King had been a communist sympathizer, the president referred to the eventual declassification of the FBI's secret recordings: "Well, we'll know in about thirty-five years, won't we?"

A Contentious Legacy

Thirty-five years have passed since Reagan said those words, yet debate over King's socialism still turns a great deal on comments delivered in private and relayed through archival records or secondhand interviews. Among the most cited are off-the-record statements that King delivered at gatherings of the Southern Christian Leadership Conference (SCLC) toward the end of his life. At a 1966 retreat in South Carolina, for example, King insisted that "something is wrong with capitalism," championed Scandinavian forms of social democracy, and argued that there must be "a move toward a democratic socialism." In his 1967 annual address to the SCLC, King declared that the civil rights movement needed to "address itself to the question of restructuring the whole of American society." For King, the fact that an

affluent society had forty million citizens in poverty meant not simply "raising a question about the economic system, about a broader distribution of wealth," but turning to "question the capitalistic economy," the ownership of capital, and the failure of markets to meet vital needs. Perhaps most famously, William Rutherford, an SCLC ally, reported that King privately told him, "Obviously we've got to have some form of socialism, but America's not ready to hear it yet."

Such statements seem to buttress the claim that King became more radical in his later years. Yet there is evidence of continuity in King's views on economic justice dating back to the late 1940s. In undated seminary writings from that period, King predicted that "capitalism has seen its best days in America, and not only in America, but in the entire world . . . it has failed to meet the needs of the masses." In a 1952 love letter to Coretta Scott, King wrote that "I am much more socialistic in my economic theory than capitalistic," and later, "I would certainly welcome the day to come when there will be a nationalization of industry."

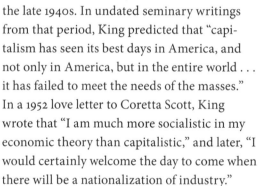

Stanley Levison

There are, however, two major difficulties with relying upon such statements to adjudicate King's "socialism." The first is that King never articulated them in his published writings, despite a career of careful, considered, and courageous statements on an astonishing range of issues. The second is that these statements contain few specifics fleshing out their relationship to traditional conceptions of socialism, including the abolition of private property or wage labor. In 1967, for example, King demanded that we ask "Who owns the oil?" or "Who owns the iron ore?" but he did not then suggest collective ownership of natural resources or utilities. It is difficult, therefore, to know what would separate King's views from those of liberals such as John Rawls, who argued for the massive redistribution of income and assets and lamented the outsized influence of profit motives and concentrated wealth in capitalist societies. Even if those who call King socialist were clearer about what they thought "socialism" entailed beyond egalitarian distribution and concern for capitalism's corrosive cultural effects, King's statements are not consistent or straightforward enough to be conclusive. We cannot establish him as a committed socialist; we also cannot prove that he wasn't one.

The Radical King Is Back

This lack of decisive evidence, however, hasn't discouraged interest in King-as-socialist. His name figures prominently in contemporary socialist writing, from Martin Hägglund's *This Life*, a new exploration of the philosophical foundations of democratic socialism, to Keeanga-Yamahtta Taylor's *From #BlackLivesMatter to Black Liberation* and Bhaskar Sunkara's *The Socialist Manifesto*. Leftist publications such as *Jacobin* and *In These Times* have solicited rafts of articles dedicated to King's place in socialist history. The self-described socialist senator and presidential candidate Bernie Sanders has especially channeled King's iconography, naming his most recent book *Where We Go From Here* after King's 1967 manifesto.

> **King thought capitalism was "like a losing football team in the last quarter trying all types of tactics to survive."**

For twenty-first-century socialists in the United States, invoking King serves two obvious needs. First, King combines a blistering critique of racism – including racism *within* the left – with an unapologetically left-wing vision of economic justice. King never minces words on the role of racism in American inequality, but he also doesn't make the mistake of reducing all black disadvantage to racial discrimination, instead foregrounding broader factors of economic transformation and public policy. This provides him with a critique of black nationalism that is useful for contemporary leftists critical of so-called "identity politics." His thoughts on this in *Where Do We Go From Here: Chaos or Community?* (1967) are worth quoting at length:

> Just as the Negro cannot achieve political power in isolation, neither can he gain economic power through separatism. While there must be a continued emphasis on the need for blacks to pool their economic resources and withdraw consumer support from discriminating firms, we must not be oblivious to the fact that the larger economic problems confronting the Negro community will only be solved by federal programs involving billions of dollars. One unfortunate thing about Black Power is that it gives priority to race precisely at a time when the impact of automation and other forces have made the economic question fundamental for blacks and whites alike. . . . In short, the Negroes' problem cannot be solved unless the whole of American society takes a new turn toward greater economic justice.

Second, King provides a powerful rejoinder to those voices that have successfully demonized socialists as anti-American and contemptuous of religious faith. Unlike this conservative caricature, King developed his most radically egalitarian and politically militant arguments with a reliance on Christian scripture and the Declaration of Independence. In the 1965 sermon "The American Dream," for example, King offers his take on American exceptionalism, proclaiming that "God somehow called

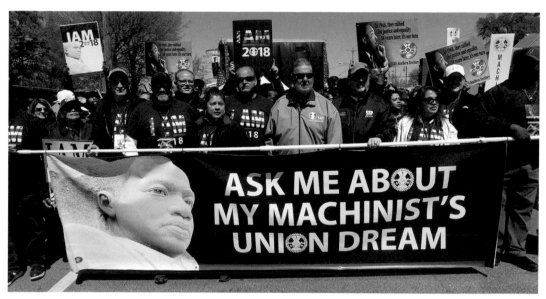

Workers march in Memphis on the 50-year anniversary of Martin Luther King Jr.'s assassination, April 2018.

America to do a special job for mankind and the world." This task, he says, demands that we uproot not only racism, but also the "class system," which "can be as vicious and evil as a system based on racial injustice."

Invoking King can be tricky, however, as Senator Sanders recently discovered. At the "She the People" Presidential Forum in Houston in April 2019, he was booed by black women for this innocuous-sounding answer to a question about combating the surge in white supremacist violence: "I was actually at the March on Washington with Dr. King back in 1963, and – as somebody who actively supported Jesse Jackson's campaign, as one of the few white elected officials to do so in '88 – I have dedicated my life to the fight against racism and sexism and discrimination of all forms." There were many factors at work in the audience's reaction, but surely some of it was a sense that Sanders's attempt to link his socialism with King smacked of political opportunism.

Grassroots Democracy

To move beyond cynicism and confusion, it might be best to stop asking whether King was a socialist, and instead ask what King the public philosopher can teach socialists today.

Two elements of King's thought seem especially important for contemporary controversies around socialism: one, his conception of democracy, and two, his demand for a "radical revolution of values."

It is striking how quickly contemporary discussions of "democratic" socialism gloss over democratic practice to focus on redistributive public policy. In doing so, they often reduce the involvement of ordinary citizens to voting and contributing to electoral campaigns. Sanders's interest in democratic socialism, for example, primarily seems to be about the *method* of redistribution (via electoral politics) and a sense that concentrated wealth unfairly devalues democratic citizenship.

Although King is known as a voting rights activist, his wider thinking on democracy is neglected. His most original reflections lay less in the sphere of formal electoral politics than in spheres of democratic action. King saw mass meetings, public arbitration, boycotts, civil disobedience, and civic association as ways to deepen and reinvigorate democratic society, above and beyond voting and legislation. Recounting the failure of Reconstruction to deliver multiracial democracy, King consistently warned that civil rights must not be treated as

permanent achievements but as perpetually vulnerable goods that need to be defended and deepened by vigilant citizen action such as boycott, protest, and civil disobedience.

One goal of state policy, King thought, should be to expand the spaces in which citizens come together to exchange ideas and resist exploitation and domination. For example, while King defended a guaranteed annual income for citizens on the grounds that it respected the dignity of persons, he also thought it might play a powerful role in fostering democratic action. A guaranteed income would allow people to resist domination by employers, bureaucrats, and landlords. Having watched defenders of the status quo in the South punitively and illegally deny employment or welfare benefits to African American activists, King forcefully objected to "uncontrolled bureaucratic or political power" across the full sweep of social life.

To resist such power, King explicitly championed forms of collective organization such as welfare and tenants' unions, local arbitration boards, and school and transportation boards. In 1967, King described these as "new methods of participation in decision-making" that could bring about a truly integrated society, where power is shared justly. Such organizations *require* the participation of the disadvantaged themselves in order to adequately recognize

their dignity and respond to their needs and perspectives, and to punish arbitrary bureaucratic humiliation and overreach.

Such ideals, King thought, could never be achieved within the boundaries of formal politics alone. They must always be supplemented by traditions of protest and by sustained civic participation. King's insistence on this is an important contribution toward what the German philosopher Axel Honneth treats as a defining aim of socialism: "a general structure of democratic participation" across the spheres of social life. This concept of distributed democratic power is fundamentally at odds with any socialism that relies on top-down, technocratic policymakers and bureaucracies to pursue its aims. King's vision does not simply seek to "break up the banks." It treats enhancing collective decision-making across the gamut of major institutions as a moral and political imperative.

A Revolution in Values

Crucially, genuine democratic participation across society would also require what King called "a radical revolution in values." American capitalism, King warned, is shot through with racism, materialism, and militarism in ways that have become structural. "A nation that will keep people in slavery for 244 years," King proclaimed in 1967, "will 'thingify' them and make them things. And therefore, they will exploit them. . . . And a nation that will exploit economically will have to have foreign investments and everything else, and it will have to use its military might to protect them. All of these problems are tied together."

Put more sharply, King's argument treats American capitalism's valuations as fundamentally irrational, self-undermining, and dangerous. They lead to war-making and rapacious profiteering, the unjust and irrational allocation of social wealth and power, and the treatment of people – especially poor and racially stigmatized workers – as *things*. As such, these precarious members of the political community have their fate determined by considerations of market efficiency rather than moral equality.

Fundamentally, however, this revolution in values needed to be justified by democracy. "If democracy," King stated, "is to have breadth of meaning it is necessary to adjust this inequity." King's way of framing these questions made it plain to his audience that the values of the existing economic order were not natural or inevitable but, as W.E.B. Du Bois put it in 1920, "strictly controlled" and "not matters of free discussion and determination." Du Bois imagined supplanting American oligarchy with the "free discussion and open determination of the rules of work and wealth and wages." Real democracy, he claimed, would place the "scientific and ethical boundaries of our industrial activities . . . in the control of the public whose welfare such decisions guide." King echoed such a vision when he challenged "a system that has created miracles of production and technology to create justice."

For King, no principle emergent from capitalism or liberalism could possibly justify the obscenity of endemic poverty alongside extravagant wealth and technological achievement. King condemned such an order, in which the political economy imposes deprivation and degradation upon citizens even in the midst of affluence, as one "as cruel and blind as the practice of cannibalism at the dawn of civilization."

King's stridency on this point is instructive. For all of the ambition of the Green New Deal or of proposals for universal health and child care, it's striking how tied up they still are with the imagination of middle-class strivings. By the end of his life, King had gone far beyond such

Great Society measures to instead declare that "the time has come for us to civilize ourselves by the total, direct, and immediate abolition of poverty." King's call to end poverty (and abolish slums) is a challenge even to self-professed democratic socialists today, insofar as it entails confronting the deep historical and racial causes of wealth inequality and rethinking the existing legal order on matters from labor rights to metropolitan boundaries. The sweeping changes these goals demand explain why King used the language of "revolution," whether he intended the word to have a socialist meaning or not.

> **We must pose fundamental questions about what, and whom, we value.**

In seminary in 1951, King thought capitalism was "like a losing football team in the last quarter trying all types of tactics to survive." "What will the new movement be called in America?" he wondered, suggesting that the aftermath of capitalism might go by "socialism, communism, or socialistic democracy." In the end, however, such terms did not matter much: "the point is that we will have a definite change."

Almost seventy years later, such confidence in a transformed future sounds unfamiliar, as if in a foreign tongue. Today we still live in a nation that, as King said in 1967, is "gorged on money while millions of its citizens are denied a good education, adequate health services, decent housing, meaningful employment, and even respect." If we want to achieve the "radical revolution in values" that King described, we must move beyond symbolic anti-racism and the rhetoric of radicalism. Taking King's example seriously would license us to dream at a scale worthy of the catastrophic challenges we face, and perhaps even to imagine a society which – from the vantage of today's disinherited – truly deserves the name "democracy." ⇝

EXPO

In Cali, Colombia, life goes on behind tinted windows: thin membranes, solid as walls, between the danger outside and the danger within.

HAROLD MUÑOZ

UNCLE JAVIER had a Toyota Land Cruiser with tinted windows. I used to take refuge there with Marcela, my cousin. The car not only had a panic button to activate an alarm that wailed like the end of the world, it also had a microphone. It was like playing with a walkie-talkie. We would punch the button and yell out the first thing that came into our heads – "Get out of the way, we've got an injured person here, let us through!" – our voices blaring out over the loudspeaker.

It was said that of all our family, the person who ran the biggest risks was my uncle Javier. I didn't really understand what that meant, but there was a reason he had that car and a mansion and a pack of Rottweilers we weren't allowed to get close to. His Toyota was a bunker. Marcela and I believed it could

Cali, Colombia, 2015. Photograph by Hilzías Salazar.

Harold Muñoz, born in Cali, Colombia, in 1992, is the winner of the Nuevas Voces *award for his novel* Nadie grita tu nombre *(Emecé, 2014). He is an editor at* El Malpensante *magazine, where this article first appeared in a Spanish version. Translated from Spanish by Kelley D. Salas.*

withstand anything: an explosion, an earth-quake, a tsunami, gunshots.

In Cali, most people tint the windows of their cars, so as to get the feeling of safety that Marcela and I used to have in her father's Toyota, or that we'd get by covering up with a sheet at night. That's how people try to survive when they feel exposed.

BACK WHEN my uncle Javier still lived in the city, my dad had a Renault 4. One day I asked him to tint the windows so that nothing would happen to us when we went out for grilled chicken or to the movies, as we often did. He answered that tinted windows were in poor taste, and that he didn't owe anything to anyone. Also, he added, people will rob you whether or not the windows are tinted. And yes: he was right then, and he's still right now. People get robbed whether or not their windows are tinted. The thieves knock on the glass with their fist or with the grip of their handgun and that's it: open sesame. They never know what they'll get; it's almost like cracking open a Kinder Surprise egg. Sometimes they get an iPhone or a big wad of cash; other times, a broken cell phone – that's fairly common now, unfortunately for the thieves. If you really want to avoid a robbery, it's more effective to carry an old cell phone to use as a decoy than it is to tint your windows. The only thing the windows do is show the thieves their own reflections without them having to see the person waiting on the other side. The victim is a mere shadow, incapable of calling for empathy. If I ever had to commit an armed robbery, I'm pretty sure I'd rather do it in front of a mirror.

> In the end, tinted windows are really there for only one reason: to cut you off from contact with the world.

But people continue to insist on their dark barriers. What used to be the mark of drug traffickers or politicians has become the norm here. In Cali, tinting your car windows is just expected, like buying a case for your cell phone. It's the trend, plus it's supposed to help with climate control: the dark glass reflects UV light from the sun. But in the end, tinted windows are really there for only one reason: to cut you off from contact with the world. How do the city and our sensations of it change if we pass through it in a blackened bubble?

YOU COULDN'T roll down the windows of my uncle's Toyota, so when he took us to the McDonald's drive-through, he had to open the door to order. We never got out of the car to eat in the restaurant, since it was more fun to eat in his mansion, in front of the home theater. My uncle would make sure there was no one suspicious around, then he'd poke his head out to speak to the woman taking orders. He'd order double for everyone – thanks to him, I got the whole collection of *Star Wars III* figurines. Then he'd give the responsibility of retrieving the hamburgers to us kids. He'd pull the Land Cruiser forward a few meters, as you do at a fast-food joint. Whoever was sitting in the left seat got the job; one day it was my turn. I opened the door of the armored vehicle, grabbed the food as fast as I could, and passed out the boxes. Because I wasn't that strong, I didn't manage to close the door all the way. Slam it harder, said my uncle's wife, if it opens, the street kids will kidnap you.

Rolling down the windows is dangerous. The proliferation of tinted glass reveals a fear of common spaces, of going out. Cali, a city of

lights, bounces off the dark panes. A car with tinted windows is a severed neuron: color is perceived differently, the noise from the street is tamed, the air conditioning filters the smells. Public areas are viewed with distrust. There's a reason most people prefer the shopping malls, which get bigger and swankier every year, to the parks and plazas. This sense of danger has estranged us from the city, filling it with black mirrors that deflect everything unwanted while we travel from point A to point B. Street vendors selling gum and candies knock on the car windows the way you'd knock on the windows of a house that's so dark inside it seems empty.

It's almost impossible now to visualize the humanity of the people who look out from behind the dark tinted windows.

DESPITE TRAFFIC LAWS that regulate how dark tinted windows can be, it's almost impossible now to visualize the humanity of the people who look out from behind them.

I remember a day when my family left the city to eat *sancocho*, a traditional Colombian dish, at a restaurant in the country. After lunch, I told my uncle that I wanted to ride back with him. He said yes, but my cousin Marcela had a different idea. She wanted to make faces at people, she told me. I had a hard time saying no to my cousin – I still do – so I agreed, and we went back to the city in my dad's Renault. We didn't know it then, but making faces at people would become one of our favorite games. This was the first time

we tried it. We drove with the windows down. The wind dried out our mouths, got in our eyes and noses. When we caught the smell of a factory or of roadkill or of a rotting sugarcane field, she'd accuse me of farting and I'd accuse her. The sun was a quivering scoop of orange sherbet, melting and dripping inside the car. Once we got into the city, we flattened ourselves against the back seat and poked our heads up against the rear window like a pair of puppets. Then we made faces at the people behind us, sticking out our tongues and crossing our eyes. They saw us, and we saw them. Some responded with a conspiratorial grin, and others gave us the finger, which made us laugh our heads off and spurred us to find new victims. We kept it up all along the streets we drove through. That day our game must have lasted an hour and a half at the most. Before she got out of the car to run to the front door of their mansion, my cousin told me she was going to ask her father to get rid of the tinted windows on his Toyota. Cars with clear windows like my dad's, she said, were just as fun.

The sun was a quivering scoop of orange sherbet, melting and dripping inside the car.

Maybe at that age she didn't sense the danger we're all in, out on the streets.

And above all, maybe the walls of her mansion kept her from recognizing the danger her father was in for doing the stuff he did.

I haven't seen my uncle Javier in ten years. One day, years before he disappeared, he sold the Toyota and bought himself a Nissan. As you'd expect, the windows were tinted even darker. ➤

Photograph by Mario Carvajal / Wikimedia Commons (public domain)

Editors' Picks

Grace Will Lead Us Home: The Charleston Church Massacre and the Hard, Inspiring Journey to Forgiveness
Jennifer Berry Hawes
(St. Martin's)

Twelve Christians at Emanuel AME Church in Charleston, South Carolina, welcomed a skinny white kid into their Wednesday night Bible study. When they closed their eyes to pray he opened fire, killing nine of them. Only two days later, at his bond hearing, several of their family members publicly forgave the shooter. Like the Amish families after the Nickle Mines school shooting, theirs was an instinctive response by people who had conformed their lives to the mind and heart of Jesus.

This astonishing act of forgiveness was neither easy nor tidy, as this compelling book shows. For one, the families did not speak as one. Many took years to forgive, others told the shooter to burn in hell. Some gradually found healing, others spiraled downward. Two daughters of Ethel Lance, who had been the glue in her fractious family, installed dueling tombstones on her grave. Meanwhile, the flood of donations and media attention led to tensions between the families and the church.

Several family members have written memoirs of their own. *Called to Forgive*, by Anthony Thompson, whose wife, Myra, led the Bible study that night, is notable for a heartfelt letter to the killer urging him to repent. Sharon Risher, one of the tombstone planters, was furious at her sister for forgiving so quickly at the bond hearing. Only after the killer was sentenced to death was she finally able to forgive, as she recounts in her own book, *For Such a Time as This*.

Hawes also presents the death sentence as a moment of closure. But nine holes remain in these families all the same. Justice does not make these wounds vanish. Neither does forgiveness, but at least it has given those left behind the power to carry on.

Underland: A Deep Time Journey
Robert Macfarlane
(W. W. Norton)

What's below us? That's the question at the heart of Robert Macfarlane's new book, *Underland*, a literary exploration of the earth's deep and mysterious places: caves, glacial crevasses, the catacombs of Paris, mines, and even the soil of Epping Forest, with its networks of flora, fauna, and fungi. During his explorations, Macfarlane meets people as varied and intriguing as the geographical features that surround them: a British ecologist named Merlin Sheldrake, a Norwegian fisherman, Slovenian peasants, and Parisian cataphiles.

Running through this delightful book like a seam of shale is the theme of humankind's relationship to nature, and the way we have, since the very dawn of civilization, transformed the features of the landscape. A visit to Greenland's glaciers, melting more rapidly each year, underscore the urgency of Macfarlane's ecological concerns. "A 'glacial pace' used to mean movement so slow as to be almost static," he writes. "Today's glaciers, however, surge, retreat, vanish." The reader comes away with a keen sense of connection – the ways humans are sustained by the planet, but also the ways we alter it.

Charged: The New Movement to Transform American Prosecution and End Mass Incarceration
Emily Bazelon
(Random House)

This book, which follows the fates of two young people caught up in the US criminal justice system, could prove to be among the most significant published this year. It doesn't just illustrate a crucial national problem – it offers a compelling case that it can actually be solved.

America imprisons nine times as many of its people as Germany and seven times as many as France. A primary culprit, Bazelon argues, is the huge discretionary influence wielded by prosecutors, from setting bail to deciding the severity of the charge and what sentence to seek. The poor, held in jail awaiting trial because they can't pay bail, are far more likely to be convicted and sent to prison, and subsequently more likely to offend again.

But in the disease may lie the cure. Since most district attorneys are elected by the people, Bazelon argues, all we need to do is elect reform-minded prosecutors who believe in the presumption of innocence, second chances, and rehabilitation.

The book tells how this approach is working, from Philadelphia to Chicago to Houston, in red and blue districts alike. This is a cause with bipartisan momentum; conservatives including the Koch brothers and Donald Trump are backing change, recognizing the costs of mass incarceration.

Though two case studies can hardly be adequately representational, Bazelon does well to keep it personal: Noura, a teenager charged with her mother's murder, and Kevin, who picked up his friend's gun as cops burst in, clearly face very different district attorneys who hold the keys to their future. And We the People hold the keys to the DA's office.

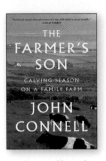

The Farmer's Son: Calving Season on a Family Farm
John Connell
(Houghton Mifflin Harcourt)

Old ways meet new and the generations work out their tensions all over again in this evocative memoir, as Connell seeks to overcome depression and anger toward his father by returning to the family farm.

Connell doesn't spare himself or us the pain of these conflicts, chiefly between himself and his father, and between the farmer's occupation and the writer's. These climax amidst the beauty of County Longford in the spring, rich in farm life's daily chores, the triumphs and the defeats and the sheer hard work. You'll learn about delivering calves and lambs, which is John's specialty, but also about the love and trust that develop between human and animal on a farm.

In John Connell, Ireland might find its Wendell Berry; *The Farmer's Son* was a number one bestseller there. It is probably even more needed in the United Kingdom, and certainly in the United States, where agriculture in general has strayed even further from its pastoral roots. It is a gentle tale, counseling humane treatment of animals and land for the sake of the whole community. Along the way, Connell drops in such fascinating historical details – whoever knew the Nazis bred a fierce wild bull to hunt in a Polish forest after they carried out ethnic cleansing there? – that we half hope the writer's vocation wins out over the farmer's. But then what would become of the gentle shepherd?
➤ *The Editors*

(continued from page 112)

suffering great One on the Cross of mankind!"
Through Buber, he began to see in Judaism as
well the outlines of a power that would draw
mankind together in a coming messianic age.
The Hasidic legends he learned, explained the
philosopher Michael Löwy
in his 1992 study *Redemption
and Utopia: Libertarian
Judaism in Central Europe*,
represented to Landauer "the
future within the present,
the spirit within history,
the whole within the individual. . . The liberating and
unifying God within imprisoned and lacerated man; the
heavenly within the earthly."

> "Jesus was a truly
> inexhaustible
> figure – so rich,
> so bountiful and
> generous."
> *Gustav Landauer*

In 1908, his period of calm at an end, he
helped to found the Sozialistische Bund, a
federation of cooperative communities. In
1911 he published *For Socialism*, the clearest
and most complete statement of his thought:
"Socialism has nothing to do with demanding
and waiting; socialism means doing."

The coming of World War I brought an
end to the Bund's activities but, even during
wartime, Landauer encouraged Germans to
live out productive cooperation: to grow food
on the borders of streets and on lawns – projects which would be schools of community.
With the armistice, an explosion of interest
in social change rocked Germany – interest
in Landauer's anarchism, and in the bloodier
game of Communist revolution. The Marxists,
he wrote in a 1910 book review, "have accustomed themselves to living with concepts, no
longer with men. There are two fixed, separate
classes for them, who stand opposed to each
other as enemies; they don't kill men, but the
concept of exploiters. . . ."

Such violence had never been Landauer's
way. "There can only be a more human
future," he once insisted, "if there is a more
humane present." But he was swept up in
the government's crackdown on anything
that smacked of dissidence.
After his murder, one of his
daughters found his body
dumped in a common grave.

But his physical death
did not kill his legacy;
his influence only grew.
Landauer's vision of a
federated network of
agrarian communities
was the blueprint for
Israel's kibbutzim; his ideas
profoundly shaped the thought of Bruderhof
founder Eberhard Arnold, prompting him in
1920 to start a community inspired in large
part by Landauer's ideals.

"What have we made of our younger generation?" Landauer asked in his 1911 call to action:

. . . cowardly little men without youth,
wildness, courage, without joy in attempting
anything. . . . But we need all that. We need
attempts. . . . We need failures upon failures
and the tough nature that is frightened by
nothing, that holds firm and endures and
starts over and over again until it succeeds,
until we are through, until we are unconquer-
able. Whoever does not take upon himself the
danger of defeat, of loneliness, of setbacks,
will never attain victory. . . . We want to create
from the heart, and then we want, if must be,
to suffer shipwreck and bear defeat until we
have the victory and land is sighted. ⤳

Gustav Landauer

JASON LANDSEL

On May 1, 1919, in the tumultuous aftermath of Germany's defeat in World War I, reactionary paramilitaries retook Munich from a group of Communists who had seized the city. They arrested a forty-nine-year-old journalist who had served as minister of culture in Munich's short-lived revolutionary government. The following morning, amid cries of "Dirty Bolshie," they beat him, shot him, and trampled him until he was dead.

Despite the soldiers' words, Gustav Landauer was no Bolshevik. The year before, he had written that the Bolsheviks were "working for a military regime which will be more horrible than anything the world has ever seen." He was something altogether different: a nonviolent anarchist who believed that the only solution to the problems of militarized, capitalistic Europe was life in voluntary communities bound together by shared work, by love, and by something else towards which he reached. For Landauer, the term "socialism" meant "a struggle for beauty, greatness, and richness of peoples" (*For Socialism*, 1911). Far from a state system imposed by force, it was to be an organic grassroots movement that would emerge as people began to live differently, "building the new world in the shell of the old."

> "The transformation of society can come only in love, in work, and in stillness."
>
> *Gustav Landauer*

Landauer was born to a middle-class Jewish family in Karlsruhe, Germany, on April 7, 1870. His generation drank deeply from the wells of German romanticism, seeking to find, in that movement's focus on the inner life, a political corrective to factories and slums and the bourgeois superficiality around them.

After college, Landauer was swept up in the cultural and political life of 1890s Berlin. He joined a theater troupe and married an actress, Grete Leuschner (they would later divorce). He also began developing the ideas that would define his philosophy: workers needed to voluntarily abandon the capitalist system and form autonomous communities. It was a vision that he repeatedly tried to live out. Upon being released from his first prison term – to which he was sentenced for his writings in *Der Sozialist* – he joined the communitarian effort *Neue Gemeinschaft*. Here he met the Jewish philosopher Martin Buber, who became a lifelong friend. A period of relative calm followed, during which he worked on translations of Shakespeare and Meister Eckhart.

Although an atheist, Landauer had long admired the figure of Christ, and wrote in *Call to Socialism* that "Jesus was a truly inexhaustible figure. . . . Where would our whole . . . machinery be without this calm, tranquil,

(Continued on preceding page)

Jason Landsel is the artist for Plough's *"Forerunners" series, including the painting opposite.*